THE
BAD DAY
BOOK™

Parenting Edition

├──────────────────┤

The Bad Day Group, LLC
Riverton, Utah

Compiled By: Amilee Weaver Selfridge
Edited By: Liz Kazandzhy
Cover Design By: Jenalee Marshall

The Bad Day Book Parenting Edition

Copyright © 2025 by The Bad Day Group, LLC

Published and Compiled by The Bad Day Group, LLC www.thebaddaybook.com

Compiled by Amilee Weaver Selfridge

Edited by Liz Kazandzhy

Cover Design by Jenalee Marshall

For Permissions contact: publisher@thebaddaygroup.com

ISBN: 979-8-9890098-7-9 (print)

Library of Congress Control Number: 2025900453

First Edition

For the parents who have said
"This too shall pass"
and then wondered why it hasn't yet.

TABLE OF CONTENTS

Have Kids, They Said. It'll Be Fun, They Said.

It Seemed Like a Good Idea at the Time

Parenting is Like Chess. I Don't Know How to Play
Chess.

You Can't Make This Stuff Up

When I was young, I just didn't get it.

No, what I *really* thought was that my *parents* didn't get it.

Some examples.

In the day of landlines, our cordless phone always went missing. One time, it went missing for days. We couldn't find it anywhere—that is, until one of my sisters went outside to get something from a freezer in our garage. Lo and behold . . . the cordless phone.

In the freezer!

And you know what? We teased my mom about it.

I didn't understand how you could possibly lose a phone in a freezer.

Then, when I was a little older, we went to cook something one Christmas. When we opened the oven, what did we find? The leftover remnants of a carved *Thanksgiving* turkey. Still in the pan!

Still in the juices! Covered in a thick, hairy mold! Just hanging out in our second oven.

And you know what? I judged.

I didn't understand how you couldn't realize you had a turkey molding in your kitchen for over a month.

I didn't spare my dad from judgment either.

One family vacation, we were visiting New York, which, of course, meant a stop at the Statue of Liberty. We boarded the ferry . . . then waved to the Statue of Liberty as we sailed past, apparently on our way to Staten Island instead.

Once again, judgments were passed.

And I remember another moment when I was nearing adulthood. As my parents and I would sit at the dinner table, I would talk and talk . . . and talk. Did I mention I would talk . . . a lot? During one such meal, my dad very kindly told me that it really wasn't necessary for me to tell them *everything* about my life.

I was baffled at why they wouldn't want to know *every* detail about my teen drama.

I bet you can see where this is going . . . the judgment zone.

But oh, how could I have been so wrong? So misled? So . . . judgmental?

The years passed, and eventually, my turn to parent came around.

Want to know how it's going?

I once changed my son's diaper, only to realize . . . my dog had a diaper on and my son didn't.

I went to make breakfast one morning and found the cereal in the fridge and the warm, chunky milk in the pantry.

On more than one occasion, my husband stopped me from trying to put a binkie or a bottle in his mouth, not the baby's.

I have sent my two sons to school with the other one's backpack . . . again, on way more than one occasion.

One December, I went outside to my garage to get something out of the fridge to make a Christmas treat. And can you guess what I found in there? Yep, a moldy pot of soup . . . from Halloween! I didn't even try to clean it—I just threw away the whole pot!

While on vacation, I took one simple wrong turn. But don't worry, it only took two extra hours to get back to the correct turn.

One day, my son, who I love with every fiber of my being, would not stop talking about Minecraft. Hours and hours every day. Every little detail. And did I respond kindly, like my dad? Nope. I accidentally burst out the words "I don't care about Minecraft!" to my poor, sweet son who just wanted to share with me what he loved so much.

Not too long ago, I lay in bed pondering my life choices. I had just stood at my back door, in the middle of the night, for almost thirty minutes, waiting for my dog to finish going to the bathroom. When she didn't return, I woke my husband to help me search the neighborhood for our missing dog.

Want to know what had really happened?

I had woken up needing to go to the bathroom. Me—not the dog. And instead of going to the bathroom, I went and opened the back door to let my dog out. But she wasn't even there! My dog lay in bed asleep for the entire hour and a half we spent trying to find her.

As I lay back in bed and realized I still had to go to the bathroom, that's when I knew I had been wrong.

And now I wonder, how did my parents always have it so together? Why could I only remember a handful of instances when parenting got the best of them when it feels like *I* have a dozen new instances every . . . single . . . day?

Seriously, parenting does something to a person.

What it all comes down to is this: Parenting should be a judgment-free zone—whether you're a child judging your parents, a parent judging yourself, or frankly, any person judging any parent.

This is a judgment-free zone. What happens in parenthood stays in parenthood.

-Amilee Weaver Selfridge

Instructions Not Included

IF YOU ONLY KNEW

Amilee Weaver Selfridge

H ER EYES SHONE WITH love and excitement, full of longing and hope for what her future held. I bet she didn't even realize she was cradling her (very pregnant) belly while watching my boys.

I had just walked into the store with them, and the young woman standing at the checkout register couldn't keep her eyes off them. I couldn't fault her—my sons were two of the cutest boys to ever walk the earth. They drew attention everywhere we went. They were on point that day too, both smiling and laughing. My older son asked everyone who passed by us for a hug, and his smiling eyes drew them all in for those hugs.

While my sons worked the room, getting the attention of every-one near us, my attention stuck on this young woman's face. Her focus on them was palpable, waves of longing flowing out of her. I knew without a doubt that this woman could not wait to be a mom. I struggled to keep back a laugh at the thought that soon enough—sooner than later based on the size of her belly and tear-rimmed eyes—she would be welcomed to the reality of parenting.

Oh, if you only knew.

I willed her to understand that parenting is so much more than those deceiving little smiles and cute faces.

Trust me. Nothing can prepare you for that moment. You'll learn, though. Soon enough. You'll know.

She waved to my boys and then gushed about how adorable they were. How their smiles made her happy. I couldn't hold back my own smile as she proclaimed they made her so excited to meet her little man within the next month. I was right.

Of course I was. I shouldn't be too proud of myself—not many people could have missed that.

For her sake, I wish the story could have ended right there. But as any parent knows, that's just not how parenting goes.

I walked into the first aisle, searching a shelf for an item I needed. Hearing some commotion, I turned around to see my younger son climbing out of the cart and onto a person walking by. I grabbed him off the unsuspecting gentleman and laughed a little while I stuck him back in the cart and continued to shop. This would not be an easy task though as he climbed onto every single person who walked by our cart, and if it wasn't a person, he climbed into their carts. I seriously could not take my eye off him for even one second.

He's lucky that smile is so darn cute.

With my focus on trying to shop, while also limiting the chaos my younger son was creating, I lost track of my older son. I couldn't see him anywhere.

Grabbing my youngest, who again was attempting to use another human as a form of escape, I went to search. But I didn't make it far before my little boy (or a rabid raccoon—not really sure which it was at this point) began wrestling me to get away.

How can someone so small be so strong?!

Despite being the strong adult that I am, I was losing. I tried putting my youngest in the cart again to cage him in, but that seemed to be the very worst choice. Instant hysterics and chaos.

He started screaming and grabbing the items, throwing them anywhere he could.

He was too fast for me. I couldn't get a hold of him. Within seconds, his hands grabbed two more items and threw them.

CRASH!

Really? How is that even possible?

In the whole cart, there had only been two glass items (had being the key word). Now they lay broken on the ground around us.

With glass and liquid spread around me, my youngest still screaming and trying to throw the rest of the items, and my oldest son missing, I frantically tried to take control of the situation.

I began yelling my oldest son's name while trying to dig through the diaper bag for something—anything—to make my youngest stop screaming.

Nothing I found would stop the screaming.

Hundreds of eyes were on us. Okay, maybe not hundreds, but at least twenty.

Take a picture, why don't you? It'll last longer. (*giggle*) That was a good one. But seriously, they sure are enjoying the free show.

I scooped up my still-screaming youngest and went searching for my oldest, who was still missing.

A few aisles later, I found him. He was happy as could be, smiling and skipping down the aisle.

Okay, we've got this. I'm going to get in control again. Wait, what are those?

In his cute little hands were at least a hundred tags. The tags stores put on the shelves that list what the item is and how much it costs.

My son, giggling, stopped and pulled off another tag from a shelf before walking away.

I shouted his name to stop. Which, of course, in his ears meant . . . run.

Oh my gosh, why is this happening to me? I try to be a good person!

With all the chaos, I couldn't even tell you what happened within the next minute.

It included a chase with my oldest, who thought we were playing the funniest game ever, while somehow lugging my screaming younger son over my shoulder.

Moments later, the three of us were standing near the entryway of the store again, my oldest now crying along with my screaming youngest. Somewhere we had left a full cart surrounded by broken jars. A trail of tags and items from my diaper bag was strewn about all along the path we had just run.

Okay, it really might be a hundred eyes now. They're getting quite the show today.

As I tried to ignore all the looks, a brave woman approached me and offered to help. She asked if she could hold my screaming youngest while I "sorted out my mess." I gratefully handed him over and went to collect our many items strewn around. I asked my older son to pick up the tags he had dropped while I got all the items from the diaper bag.

Suddenly, it went quiet!

She's a miracle worker! How did she get him to stop crying?

I breathed a sigh of relief as I picked up the last of our mess. (Okay, the last of *this* mess.)

As I stood back up, I looked at the brave woman holding my son just in time to see him gagging.

Oh, please no!

And before anything could be done, he threw up all over the sweet angel who had helped us.

I just froze, joining the onlookers at eyeing the chaos all around me.

Oh, sweet mercy. Why me?

A man, with two children of his own, broke the silence with an escaped laugh.

He looked around apologetically before he turned to walk away, all while giving me a knowing look.

See. He knows. He gets it.

There were some towels on a shelf by me. I grabbed two, mimicking my son by tearing the tags off.

I handed one directly over to my son's unfortunate victim, then wrapped my youngest son, who had taken up crying again, in the other one.

Slipping my oldest son's hand into mine, I approached the pregnant worker at the register.

It's time for this show to be over.

Over the noise of both my sons crying, I paid for the two towels and apologized for the mess and cart we had left . . . somewhere. I got the tags from my oldest son and handed them to the pregnant young woman, not even knowing how to apologize for the trouble we had left behind.

The last thing I saw as I walked out of the store was her eye, darting between the tags in her hands and my boys. A bit of shock. A lot of overwhelmed fear.

Again, I held back a laugh.

Mission accomplished.

Feeling a little bad about bursting her hopeful bubble so soon, I decided it was a good lesson for her. The sooner you know, the better.

Some days, they truly are lucky that their smiles are so cute.

OF CANNIBALS AND MICE

Robert Runté

WHEN MY DAUGHTER WAS fourteen, she was in an advanced academic program at school, active in theater evenings and weekends, and prone to insomnia. The night before a major exam, I found her awake and anxious. I jumped to the obvious conclusion that she was worried about the exam, and she confirmed there was a small chance she might only score 95% if she didn't spend the next two hours cramming.

I immediately launched into my "it's not about the grades" speech, followed by my lecture on "work/life balance." (Yes, I know, my parenting style was perhaps a bit too lecture-oriented, but I was a university professor, so . . . yeah.) I was about to launch into my "you need to stop cramming and go to sleep so you'll be well-rested for the exam" speech when my daughter interrupted to say that it wasn't about the exam at all. Cramming was just a way to keep her mind off what was actually worrying her.

I immediately jumped to the worst suspicions. Oh no! Did that creepy kid in the theater group try something on with her? I knew that jerk was going to be trouble!

"One of the kids at school was showing this video."

Oh no! That sounded bad. "Yes? It's okay. You know you can talk to me about anything. I'm here for you."

"Cannibals. It's kind of freaking me out."

Not where I thought this was going—and not a problem for which I had a ready-made lecture. I was somewhat incredulous.

"You're not seriously telling me you're afraid cannibals are going to break in while you're asleep and attack you?"

She held up her thumb and index finger separated by a hair. "Little bit."

She allowed the fear was irrational, but she couldn't get over the feeling that there was someone hiding just out of sight, waiting for her to go to sleep.

I recognized the cannibalism motif was simply the lightning rod for a generalized existential panic brought on by ridiculous amounts of homework, too much extracurricular activity, and all the social challenges of adolescence. So I sat down on the edge of her bed and started to talk her down by taking her fears seriously. I pointed out that (a) our house had a good alarm system to alert security if any cannibals attempted unauthorized entry; (b) our large black dog would immediately attack any intruders, and they would be the ones eaten, not her; and (c) I would be sleeping right upstairs and would hear if she cried out.

She acknowledged this was all true and reassuring, and she showed signs of maybe calming down enough to sleep.

At which point, the aforementioned large black dog burst into the bedroom, smashed into the wall, and tore her shelving apart to get at a wicker basket there. The dog was in psycho-killer mode.

As one may imagine, this was not entirely conducive to the calming tone I was trying to cultivate.

A moment later, a tiny jet-black mouse made a break for it, sprinting across the floor and out the door while the dog gave murderous chase. From behind me, standing on the bed, I heard my daughter shrieking, "I knew it! I knew there was something in here with me!"

"Well, it's gone now," I said, trying for damage control. Before I'd even finished the sentence, the dog was back, attacking the wicker basket once again.

I grabbed the damaged basket away from the dog, but before I could put it out of reach, I saw another (this time gray) mouse racing frantically around the basket as I inadvertently tipped it. Being the macho, heroic protector I am, I shrieked loudly and dropped the basket. The dog plunged her head back in and proceeded to smash the remnants to kindling in an attempt to get the terrified creature. Jaws abruptly snapped shut, and the dog trotted out of the room with the deliberate gait of an executioner.

Behind me, my daughter shouted, "Don't let her kill it! The mouse did nothing wrong!"

As I mumbled something about mouse trespass and the death penalty, I followed the action outside the bedroom in time to see a bullet-fast mouse (I was unclear if this was a third individual or if one of the previous two somehow escaped from the jaws of death) scuttle under the sitting-room piano—and my 60-pound dog kamikaze into the room nanoseconds after. As I called the dog back from battering the piano pedals, I felt that my little nighttime pep talk could have definitely gone better.

This was not, I'm sorry to confess, the only problematic encounter with mice in the house. On another occasion, I had set a few traps to catch suspected intruders in the kitchen, with reassurances to the children that it was a "catch and release" program. This worked relatively effectively, actually setting a few mice loose in the coulees, until I noticed one trap had inexplicably disappeared. Assuming I had just misremembered where I placed it, or that the dog had nosed it away somewhere, I forgot about it. A couple of days later, I was playing with my younger daughter in her room when she reached behind her into her stack of stuffies to pull out—you guessed it—a dead mouse. Unfortunately, her collection of stuffies included three plush and somewhat realistic mice, so we both sat there staring at the dead mouse for ten seconds before realizing that this one was real. (Well, the attached trap should have been a giveaway.) Why and how the mouse had dragged itself and the trap all the way across the house to my youngest's bedroom and buried itself in her stuffie collection I will never know, but her reaction was predictably hysterical.

Still, could have been worse. Could have been cannibals.

To Lie or Not to Lie? What a Question!

Jan Cauffiel Zinn

I said I would never lie to my kids. How do you teach honesty if you don't model it? Truth always wins out in the end anyway. I will not lie to my children.

Then I had kids.

You know that phrase "The truth, the whole truth, and nothing but the truth"? Does two out of three count? The "whole truth" is the one I stumble over. There are lies of commission and lies of omission, but the latter is not really a lie . . . right?

The biggest test of a parent's commitment to honesty has to be Santa Claus. When December first came along and my ten-year-old said he wanted to ask me something and I had to promise to tell the truth, I suspected the day I was dreading had arrived. I was right.

This was the conversation:

RC: "Mom, I've been wondering about something, and I really need you to be honest." (Said with great sincerity . . .)

Me: "Okay." (Heart rate rising, brain going into hyperdrive . . .)

RC: "Do you ever wrap up a package and write 'To RC from Santa' on the tag?"

Me: "Are you sure you want to know that answer, RC?" (Buy time to think, buy time to think . . .)

RC: "I'm sure."

Me: "Really sure?" (Buy more time to think . . .)

RC: "Really sure."

Me: "Well, you understand that no one is ever exactly certain what Santa means by 'good behavior,' right?"

RC: "You mean like, how good is good enough for Santa?"

Me: "Exactly." (Sharp kid.)

RC: "So, do you ever do that?" (Persistent kid.)

Me: "Well, there have been some years when I was worried that your behavior wasn't good enough for Santa, and I hated the idea of nothing being under the Christmas tree for you. So just in case . . . yes, I wrapped a gift and wrote on the tag 'To RC from Santa.'"

With a great sigh of relief, he hugged me and said, "Thank you, Mom!"

And that lie of omission survived for one more year.

The Standing Joke in the Family

Sunayna Pal

M Y HUSBAND WAS OCCUPIED with an upcoming project deadline when I reached a stage where I believed our son was primed for potty training. The summer was fading, and I decided to take the plunge solo. After all, what did I have to lose?

Our almost-three-year-old had endured short diaper-free periods, which I dubbed "brief-brief time." However, he had never quite felt the urge to pee during these intervals. Following the sage advice of my experienced parent friends, I decided to introduce him to the small potty for a few minutes after his diaper-free breaks.

I thought cleaning the small and separate potty would be too much work for me, and my borderline OCD tendencies nudged me toward an alternative solution: placing a cushioned seat atop the regular toilet, hoping for everything to fall into place, so to speak.

One evening, after a long diaper-free break, I unveiled the plush potty seat to my son. I let him hold and inspect the seat. "See the ducks on this seat? Aren't they pretty?"

He nodded with intrigue.

Pressing down on the cushion, I continued, "Also, see—it's so soft. Shall we sit and try it out? You can sit on it like Mommy." I placed it on the toilet and gently lifted him onto the cushioned throne. He squirmed slightly, trying to get comfortable on this unfamiliar seat. Yay! It seemed like we were heading in the right direction. But alas, he didn't feel like peeing. After five minutes of sitting, legs dangling, and surveying the surroundings, he announced, "Me come done now?"

"Sure, of course, sweetheart." I brought him down. "We'll try this tomorrow."

On the second day, he sat comfortably and didn't wiggle as much. He sat for over ten minutes but nothing happened. I felt a little defeated. Potty training was going to be harder than I thought.

On the third day, I encouraged him to sit and explained again the concept of him doing his business over here and not in the diaper. Then I heard the delightful sound of success. He piddled. Yippie! He was more relieved than happy (no pun intended). We celebrated by opening a pack of M&Ms. He was fascinated with the small colorful sweet spheres. I let him choose his color and he chose yellow. Perfect!

I was delighted. I had done it. Technically he did it, but you know . . . I was the one who cheered him on and made it happen. I couldn't wait to tell my husband. But he came home late and left before we woke up.

It was Wednesday and I decided to wait until Saturday to tell him. Why tell when you can show? I could surprise him. I was getting close to the "no diapers ever again" stage.

On the fourth day, I crossed my fingers. I explained the concept to my son again and told him we would celebrate with candy. And it worked! I was excited for him to be potty-trained and started planning his next diaper-free break. The happiest day of my life would be when I could get rid of his diapers.

It was a little difficult to lift him every time and make him sit on the seat, but I was happy that he was getting the hang of it. Diapers would soon be history. I had waited all my life for this moment (umm, well . . . his whole life).

Finally, Saturday arrived, and my husband had a day off. I patiently waited until and through my son's diaper break. After this, I sat my son on the potty and told him to wait. "Let's call Daddy. He'll be thrilled to see you pee. And then we can eat two candies."

My son and I called for him together, "PAPA, come quickly!"

He hurried to the bathroom and asked worriedly, "What's wrong?"

"Nothing," I reassured him, grinning. "Satu wants to show you something." Right on cue, my son began to pee.

It couldn't have been more perfect than this. I told him to wait, and Satu waited. I finished the sentence and he peed. What more could I ask for? Thank you, Lord!

After my son was done, he beamed at his dad, sporting the broadest grin I had ever seen. Just witnessing his joy filled me with pride as I looked at my husband. But his puzzled reaction was far from what I had anticipated.

I prodded, "Did we just achieve the Super Bowl of parenting, or what?"

Scratching his head, he replied, "Why is he sitting? Boys can stand and pee, no?"

Needless to say, my son's successful potty training continues to be a standing joke (pun entirely intended) in our family.

THE LONE SHOE

Jesse Neve

I USED TO WONDER what the story was when I would see a lone shoe on the side of the road. I couldn't imagine how a person could lose just one shoe and not be on the lookout for it or know how they had lost it. But after twenty-two years of motherhood, I no longer wonder . . .

When my son Jonathan was seven, I picked the kids up from school every day. In the cold Minnesota winters, they would clomp out of the school dressed in their full snowstorm gear—snow pants, hats, mittens, and boots. But the five-minute drive home was much too long in our toasty van. Jonathan always stripped down to his short sleeves as soon as he entered the van. On this specific day, we had some books to return at the local library, so I pulled up to the book drop and Jonathan happily opened the van's sliding door to drop the books in the slot.

Nothing seemed out of the ordinary, so we continued our drive home. Jon gathered his backpack and winter gear and headed inside. The next morning, in our rush to get out the door to school, we were missing a boot. We all knew he had it when he came skipping out of school yesterday. But we looked everywhere. After school, we headed back to the library. Unshockingly enough, his boot was in the library's lost and found box. Apparently, it had fallen out at the book drop, and it got to stay in the library parking lot overnight.

The next summer, we were missing one of his sandals for over a week. They were his favorite bright green Crocs. We even checked the library's lost and found, just to make sure. One day when we were leaving the high school for his sister's practice, we noticed something bright green in the ditch by the entrance to the school.

"Jon! Is that your shoe?" He hopped out of the van at the corner and ran down into the ditch to see. Yes, indeed. We have no idea how it got there.

Our last shoe issue was when all six of us arrived at the water park for a fun day of waterslides and alpine slides. My younger son Daniel, age six at the time, only arrived with one shoe. Not a big deal as far as the waterslides, but shoes were required for the alpine slides. Luckily, we were able to trade shoes back and forth with his siblings so everyone could take turns riding. But we knew he wore his shoes into the van that morning!

Well, there it was, right there in the garage when we returned home that evening. How it managed to "jump" from the car before we even drove out, we will never know.

So you see, shoes obviously have a mind of their own. And there's likely an odd turn of events that leads to that one lone shoe alongside the road that you pass every day.

Poop and Other Explosions

Trisha Simone

T HE BROWN STAIN CLUNG to the living room wall with tenacity.

A sniff of the paper towel confirmed my suspicion—poop! I whipped my head left, seeking the source. Confronted by dimples, blond curls, and big brown eyes, I exhaled. My son was playing quietly with blocks on his mat. I sidled over and lifted the back hem of his shirt.

Gasp!

Soft, stinky stool squeezed over the rim of his Pull-Ups. I gazed at his innocent smile, determined to remain calm.

"Why didn't you tell me that you had caca?" I asked.

All he said was "No bath!"

Sigh.

I whisked him towards the nearest shower. He made his displeasure known, shrieking his favorite word "No!" over and over. I ripped off all the soiled items, threw them into the sink, and closed the door to thwart his efforts to escape. I kissed and hugged him and reassured him that everything was okay. I explained that we just needed to wash off the yucky stuff. Unconvinced, he struggled to get free and refused to cooperate.

I finally got him to calm down a bit when I sprayed his backside with warm water. Giggling, he decided to go along with the impromptu washing. But his calm was temporary. He realized that something was off. This was not the normal bath routine. One by one, he began to name toys that he wanted—needed—right now!

Baby shark, mama shark, duckie, red boat, green boat, penguin. All these things were upstairs in his bathroom, of course. I only managed to distract him by singing his favorite songs at the top of my lungs.

After the frenzied shower-bath, I scurried around inspecting the carpet. Holding my breath, I begged for the thick tan pile to be free from excrement. When I was satisfied that the carpet was clean, I returned to scrubbing and disinfecting the walls.

Over the annoying music of Gabriel's toy, I heard banging on the door. It was immediately followed by short and long notes from the doorbell, like Morse code. I raced to the window to see a man in uniform.

Before I could even fully open the door, he said, "You have to leave now!"

I stared at him. "What?!"

He explained that his team was drilling nearby and hit a gas line. They had to evacuate the entire subdivision until the city inspector determined the risk of an explosion.

"Explosion?!"

I always kept snacks and a change of clothing in the stroller basket, so I grabbed the keys and bolted out of the house with my son. Thankfully, there's a park within walking distance. I fled over the sidewalk, pushing the stroller like a maniac.

At the far side of the athletic field, I let my son out to play. I called my husband, warning him to avoid the house. He said he would make a few phone calls to find out more.

Oblivious to my panic, my two-year-old ran and climbed around the playground. I kept up with him, doling out my usual words of encouragement and caution.

But I never lost sight of the line of houses that border the park. Having watched way too much television in my lifetime, I braced for a massive explosion.

The weather was uncharacteristically mild for spring in Arizona. We were comfortable. After a long wait, my husband called to announce that it was all clear. Repairs had been completed and there was no danger of explosions.

When the car arrived to take us back to the house, I opted to push the stroller home. It was easier than emptying the trunk. Calmed by a flurry of hugs, I laughed at myself for having been so afraid.

Ambling the short distance home, I savored the glorious orange sunset that burned in the sky, happy to be alive. I relished the beauty of the mundane.

I made it all the way back to my front door before I noticed the brown stain on the side of my dress.

How to Raise a Daughter

Steve Denehan

I would burp
she would laugh
we would look at each other
smiling

I would burp again
she would laugh again
it never got old
until it did

Now when I burp
she rolls her eyes
so I blame her
and she laughs

But I know
that this won't last long
and honestly
I don't know where to go from here

IT'S ALL FUN AND GAMES UNTIL . . .

"Go for it. She said she wanted to get her hair colored."

The White Lie

Tammy Brown

WHAT SHOULD HAVE BEEN a beautiful day at the park turned into a fight for control over the slide, featuring two children around two years old. One of those children was my daughter, Haley, and she was not having a good time. The park was small, but there were many sections of the playground that should have appealed to the two children. However, neither child was willing to move beyond the green bumpy slide.

The other child was a stranger, and since many families had decided to visit this particular playground on that sunny day, I wasn't sure which mom he even belonged to. Most of the moms there were using their time to relax on the benches surrounding the play area, but since I knew my child had not yet developed a healthy fear of risky events, I stuck a little closer.

In fact, I think I was the only adult who saw the power struggle over the slide, and since the altercation merely consisted of an occasional shove, there was no reason for anyone to intervene. I have always believed that in some situations, it's healthy to let children resolve their own conflicts, so I just observed the interaction of these two toddlers and provided no adult guidance.

Time after time, I saw Haley land at the bottom of the slide and then immediately run to the ladder so that she could have another turn before her temporary nemesis could. Then I watched her competitor perform the same movements to try to cast his dominance over my daughter. Occasionally, they would meet at the top of the slide, and there would be a little bit of pushing and a little bit of toddler-speak before one person would win and get to go down the slide before the other one.

Watching the two toddlers in their earnest pursuit over the slide's ownership was quite entertaining, so instead of encouraging Haley to move to the swings or monkey bars, I just watched it all unfold. After about ten minutes, Haley must have decided to use a different tactic to get the slide to herself, and I heard my daughter tell her new rival something that accomplished this goal.

"Your mama said you have to go home."

Hearing this, her rival went down the slide and went over to the benches where several moms were talking. Confused, I looked at Haley, then at the group of moms. Could she have seen his mom beckon him?

After a quick assessment, I realized there was no way she could have even known which mom was his. Even if she did, the mom group he approached was deeply involved in conversation and didn't look ready to leave anytime soon. That meant that I had just witnessed my daughter, who had been talking for less than a year, not only tell her first lie but do so with skill.

Yes, my sweet little two-year-old had come up with a creative way to solve her problem that day, a solution that didn't involve the normal physical confrontation that most toddlers utilized. There was no biting or kicking, just one sweet little voice whispering a little white lie to get her way.

And she did, indeed, get her way—because although the little boy continued to play at the park, he accepted his defeat over that part of the playground. I spent the rest of my time that day watching my crafty two-year-old enjoy sliding all by herself.

Bringing Back a Classic Hit

Jesse Neve

W HEN MY BOYS WERE four, six, and eight, the "in" thing to say was "Oohhh!" when someone was about to be reprimanded or get in trouble. For instance, I would come around the corner and see Daniel with his hand in the cookie bin right before supper and I would say, "Daniel! We're going to eat soon!" and Jon, from the other room, would yell, "Oohhh!"

Or I would see a trail of mud and dirt across the laundry room floor and yell, "Jon! Come and clean up your mess!" And from Daniel, rooms away, I would hear, "Oohhh!"

It was walking the line of disrespectful and mean in a way I couldn't really explain, and I didn't like it. Finally, I decided, "Okay, guys, the next person to use 'Oohhh!' is going to be in big trouble! We're done with it."

Later that day, I heard a splat! in the kitchen. I rounded the corner to see Ben standing by a puddle of spilled orange juice. Jon apparently had heard it from the other room too, and he arrived at the kitchen simultaneously. Out of habit, he responded, "Oohhh . . ." but then remembered as he saw my head turn toward him. With a quick raise of his eyebrows, he continued:

". . . Susannah! Oh, don't you cry for me, for I come from Alabama with my banjo on my knee!" Jon did a casual little jig as if he was just passing by, singing an old classic tune. He joyfully hummed the tune all the way up the stairway and out of sight.

Steaming Apricot Soup

Rose Florian

M Y DAD WAS A man of many talents. The two that remain in my memory are his wonderful organic garden and his delicious cooking and baking skills.

One early spring day in the late 1970s, I had returned home from work.

As was my usual habit, I went into the house, greeted my mom, then went back out to greet my dad who was always in his garden.

Approaching the garden, I noticed an odd sight. Just before the garden, Dad kept a compost heap and a rain barrel. What baffled me was that steam was rising up from the compost heap. Oh no! Fire?!

I ran into the garden and found Dad stooping, weeding the tomato plants.

"Dad! Dad!" I called out. "The compost heap is on fire!"

"For crying out loud, it's not on fire," he replied, rolling his eyes. "What's the matter with you?"

"But there's steam rising up from it! What's going on?"

Dad stood up and said, "I'll tell ya what's going on! All afternoon, all afternoon I spent cooking minestrone soup for you and Mama. I fried the hamburger with onions, green peppers, and garlic. Steamed carrots and green beans, all from my garden. Then I boiled up some of those noodles you like. Then I mixed it all together. I got two bags of the tomatoes I froze, set them aside to thaw. When they were thawed out, I added them to the soup and reheated it. I mixed everything together, but something didn't smell right. So I took a taste of the soup."

At that moment, Dad made his ready-for-war face—big eyes, face scrunched up and red as a ripe tomato. His hands clenched into fists.

"Those two bags of tomatoes I thawed?" he continued. "They weren't tomatoes, no sir! They were apricots. APRICOTS! I whipped that pan off the stove, ran out the door, and threw that rotten soup, pan and all, right on top of the compost heap. That's what you thought was on fire!"

"Um, oh gee . . . yikes. Sorry, Dad."

That night, Dad, Mom, and I had grilled cheese sandwiches for supper. Dad was completely silent with his head down, chewing his sandwich and drinking his coffee. It was obvious he was still stewing from the apricot soup disaster.

While eating, Mom and I did all we could to withhold our laughter. We didn't dare look at one another, knowing that laughing at Dad when he was mad was forbidden.

When Dad finally finished eating, he got up, went to the sink, and rinsed off his dishes. He thrust open the kitchen door and left.

I got up from the table, looked out the window, and saw that he was returning to the garden.

Sitting back down with Mom, we were finally able to look at each other. Then the uncontrollable laughter shot out of us, complete with snorting, choking, and endless tears. It was quite some time before we were able to get up and clear off the table.

Two or three weeks later, Dad seemed to have put the apricot soup disaster far behind him.

One Saturday morning, I woke up to the aroma of freshly brewed coffee that Dad had made. I said good morning to him and sat down at the kitchen table with Mom. Dad poured us all a cup of coffee, added milk to Mom's cup, and put milk and one sugar in mine.

Dad took a sip of his coffee and began reading the newspaper. Mom and I were talking about this and that. She took a sip of her coffee and winced. Too hot, I thought. I took a sip of mine and gagged.

"Mom, this coffee is horrible!" I exclaimed. "Ugh!"

"I know," she replied. "Maybe the milk went sour."

She reached for a spoon, stirring the coffee, and up came a squishy brown object. She jumped and flipped the object onto the table, spilling some of the coffee. I got up and poured mine into the sink. The same awful, squishy object was in mine.

"Dad, what kind of coffee is this?" I demanded to know.

He looked at me, then Mom.

"Apricot coffee, Dearie."

Finally, we all had one good laugh together.

SLICE OF LIFE

Anna Remennik

As our Passover surprise:
    Lice, lice, lice, lice

Crawling right before our eyes
    Lice, lice, lice, lice

Oh the horror! Oh the crisis!
Lots and lots of lousy lices!

Comb them out once, twice, thrice
    Lice, lice, lice, lice

Get them gone at any price!
    Lice, lice, lice, lice

This shampoo or that device
    For the lice, lice, lice

Will four bottles-full suffice
    For the lice, lice, lice?

Kill them all dead in a trice!
    (Lies,! lies! lies! lies!

See a doctor, if you're wise
 For the lice, lice, lice)

Vacuum this, put that on ice
 Lice, lice, lice, lice

Torch the house, is my advice
 With the lice, lice, lice

What fell thing's transpired here,
Causing all to disappear?

What great war or dire trouble
All reduced to ruin and rubble?

What titanic cataclysm
Has destroyed life's peaceful rhythm?

Echo somberly replies:
 Lice. . . lice. . . lice. . . lice. . .

SURVIVING KINDERGARTEN

Mary Traynham

M Y SON TYLER WAS excited to begin Kindergarten. He had been in school for three weeks when he ran to me outside, excitedly calling "Mama!" He came up close, lowered his voice, and said "I know what the F-word is!"

Now, I knew he would be in contact with older children on the school bus, but I was not expecting this. He excitedly said, "You want me to tell you?" Not interested in hearing ugliness from the lips of my firstborn, I said no. He could not be dissuaded and said, "I'm going to tell you anyway. It's FART!" It took all my self-control to suppress a laugh or a grin. I replied, "I won't tell anybody if you won't!"

Kindergarten was quite a year. He had gotten accepted into a magnet school housed in an old high school building that had been the first school in the area to be desegregated. The high school had long been closed, and the building hadn't been used for a while when the magnet program was introduced and the school building was repurposed into an elementary school. The cafeteria, for some reason known only to those who constructed it, had a two-inch metal pipe that protruded out of the floor up about two and a half inches, then curved over horizontally with the floor about four inches, and then capped off. The cafeteria was a busy place, with very little time for each class to go through the line, see the cashier at the other end, and then join classmates at their assigned tables.

Kindergarteners are trying so hard to be like the big kids and are pleased to carry their trays.

One day, a few months into Kindergarten, Tyler came home and said he didn't enjoy his lunch. When I asked why, he said after he saw the cashier and took his tray to join his friends, he had tripped on this protruding pipe. Never saw it with the tray obscuring his view. Fell down on top of the tray. His face went right into his pizza.

The teacher assistant was closest to him and came over. Grabbed a big handful of his hair and lifted his head out of the pizza. Then picked up a spoon and began scraping the pizza sauce and cheese off his face. Didn't help him up. He heard her say as she was returning to her duty station, "We need to get that fixed!"

Pretty, Productive, and Tomato-Like

Erika Hoffman

B ECAUSE I'M A WRITER, I'm always on the lookout for hints to improve the quality or quantity of my writing. Also, I want to convey helpful writerly guidelines to students I teach, such as those in OLLI (Osher Lifelong Learning Institute).

In one week, I received two emails with similar messages. The first had bullet points attributed to R. L. Stine. Number six was "Set a timer for 13 minutes. Write something—anything—until the timer goes off. When it dings, if writing is going well, set it for another 13 minutes. If it's not going well, leave and do something else for the next 13 minutes; then return." I contemplated the use of a timer and thought how I need one—not for writing but for chores. It's difficult for me to make myself vacuum, dust, or clean commodes—for even five minutes.

After pondering this advice, I ran across a blog from an author's web page advocating the benefits of using a "pomodoro," a little "tomato-looking" timer. So I googled "pomodoro" and saw a zillion of them on Amazon.

This kitchen timer, shaped like a cute, little, red tomato, is a time management device. It breaks work into segments of twenty-five minutes each. Then there's a pause. Pomodoro is the Italian word for "tomato," and this timer method was named by Francesco Cirillo who used it while a university student. He coined the phrase "Pomodoro Technique," which is good for perfectionists and procrastinators alike.

I ordered five. I was thinking about my young grandchildren who could use it to time their chores, tablet viewing, or homework completion. Anyway, two grandkids were coming soon with one parent each to see us for a long weekend. I'd give them each this inexpensive, practical gadget, which I thought was a better souvenir of their visit than the usual junk I waste money on.

My son flew in from New York with his seven-and-a-half-year-old daughter, Georgia, who was finishing first grade. My daughter flew in from Michigan with her almost five-year-old son, Zane, who would start kindergarten soon. Both kids seem precocious. (I know that all grandparents say that, but it's true in my case.)

Anyhow, my granddaughter was intrigued by my playing Wordle; therefore, I showed her how it worked, and we did multiple ones till her dad said, "No more. Go to bed." She pled for ten more minutes, so I thought, "Voilà!" I pulled out one of the pomodoros that had just arrived at our garage door that afternoon. She smiled, delighted by the ticking timer. I handed my grandson one too, which was still in the box. He glanced at the red plastic tomato in Georgia's hand and waved it away. "Nah."

"That's fine, Zane," I said. "It's not been opened. Georgia can take it home tomorrow and give it to her younger brother, who's also starting school in the fall."

The next day, parents and grandkids had packed to leave. Georgia carried her ticking pomodoro in her hand. I told her to put it in her suitcase or backpack. I had her take a pomodoro for her brother too. She slid it in, near her three-ring binder of Pokémon cards.

We zoomed down I-40 to the airport. I assured them we seldom had long delays at the Raleigh-Durham Airport and repeated how all the TSA folks are pleasant here in North Carolina, unlike at many other airports.

I kissed my two grandkids goodbye and hugged my son and daughter. I told them to give my best to their spouses and the rest of their young kids. I departed, proud of myself for the good time I showed these older grandchildren and their parents on this fun, five-day vacation with us.

That night, my daughter called to tell me she was back in Michigan. No problems with their flight.

"I hope your brother and Georgia had an easy flight to New York City."

"He didn't phone you?"

"No. Why, what happened?"

"Georgia put her backpack on the conveyor belt at the security gate, and TSA flagged it. They took it off to inspect it."

"Huh?" I gulped.

"Georgia started bawling. She thought they were messing with her Pokémon cards."

"What?"

"She kept screaming at her dad that it was all his fault."

"How's that?"

"I don't know. The TSA kept staring at Henry while his daughter had a meltdown."

"Oh my." My mind raced, thinking about why they were plucked out of line to have their belongings searched.

"It was awful."

"What caused it? What was suspicious?" I asked, trying to wrap my mind around why TSA swooped in on a little girl's backpack.

"I told Georgia it was just a random check. They do that sometimes," my daughter said.

"Uh-huh. You're right. Sometimes they even pick the least suspicious person to pat down." I thought about telling her how the TSA often wants to pat down my back because they claim they see something on the X-ray machine. "There's nothing there but back fat!" I've told TSA in other airports many times.

"Henry didn't think it was random."

"Oh no," I said, feeling nauseated. Suddenly, I remembered the ticking tomato tracker in Georgia's backpack.

"Henry thought the Pokémon cards caused them to search the bags."

"Hmm," I said, sighing a bit too loudly. "Who knows? A mystery indeed." I exhaled. "Maybe it was the cards. They are shiny. Well, bye!" I said quickly and hung up the phone.

Dang! This is what happens when grandmas think they've come up with a good idea—an inspired notion for a memento with a purpose. The best-laid plans of mice and men . . . well, parents and grandparents know how that goes.

Who would've guessed that a writing aid could cause such a ruckus?

In Ecclesiastes 3:4, we read, "A time to cry and a time to laugh, a time to mourn and a time to dance." That airport scuttlebutt was . . . a time of grief. Years later, when the trauma of the pomodoro catastrophe has faded, perhaps I'll finally share my ruminations about my culpability in the TSA snafu. Maybe I'll save it for Georgia's wedding toast?

SING WITH YOUR HEART

Bien Santillan Mabbayad

WHENEVER I ENSLAVED MYSELF at work in front of the computer, my seven-year-old son would accompany me, snuggling and fidgeting like a bored kitten.

Then one day, he started singing. It was one of those ridiculous songs he kept on playing on YouTube that can get stuck in your head for days. And the way he was singing it made it sound worse. He was blaring, changing his tone and inflection with every few words. He was singing it out of tune, which, I suspect, was intentional.

I tried to concentrate, typing down my notes for next week's class as much as I could, thinking it would pass. But the longer I tried ignoring him, the louder he got. It came to a point where it was too unbearable. So I stopped what I was doing and looked at him sternly. "Will you please stop singing?" I said with a strained, controlled voice. "I'm trying to concentrate here."

Then he looked up at me with his cute, round, puppy eyes and said, "But that's what my heart is telling me. I'm supposed to sing what I feel."

That shut me up. Who can counter an argument like that?

It's All Fun and Games

Amilee Weaver Selfridge

M Y SON AND I love to play games with each other. Mario Kart, checkers, and all forms of Uno, to name a few.

One of our favorites, though, is called . . . breakfast.

It goes like this.

Every morning, as early as possible, he begs and pleads for breakfast.

Since this usually starts in the middle of the night, we go through this step for several hours.

He really gets into the game and throws around statements like:

"Mom, I can't make it a second longer! I'm not going to survive any more time with no food. You're killing me!"

"Mom, people can't live like this. It's wrong."

"It has been days since you fed me."

We often even get some tears at this point in the game.

Then, after what he feels is years, I make him breakfast.

Then we switch positions.

For the next couple of hours, it's my turn to beg and plead.

I throw out statements like:

"You begged me to make this. Come eat it!"

"You said you were hungry. Just eat something."

"Please eat your breakfast. If you never eat, you might get sick."

Then finally, after what I feel is decades, he takes his last bite and straightway asks if he can have lunch now.

It's a fun game. Definitely right at the top with our favorites. I highly recommend trying it out.

WE'RE SORRY

Jesse Neve

A BUSY COUNTY ROAD runs right behind our house. Thankfully, the prior owners had enough foresight to build an eight-foot-high wooden fence between our house and the road, protecting us from noise and danger.

Earlier that autumn day, I had driven on that road, right past our fence, and I had noticed a collection of detritus strewn across the road—leaves, sticks, pieces of bark. I didn't really think too much about it. Perhaps a tree-trimming truck had spilled some of its cargo.

Ever since our four children were old enough to play outside on their own, it had been a standing rule that they stay on our side of the fence. Always. If a ball or Frisbee ended up going over the fence, they always asked an adult to retrieve it. This rule was so ingrained in their being that when their teenage cousin visited and a ball was lost, they were scandalized and came running to report that he dared venture to the other side of the fence alone to retrieve the ball.

It had been a lovely fall afternoon. It was one of those days where kids in their sparkly-clean new tennis shoes look longingly out the school windows, and the teachers grasp at the kids' attention while secretly wishing they were still on summer break as well. It was the second week of school, but the summer-like weather had continued.

As soon as everyone was home from school, and had downed the obligatory snack, they had run straight outside to play. Any homework or spelling words would have to wait for later—there were balls to kick and places to run!

That evening, as I finished cleaning up after dinner, I looked forward to grabbing a lawn chair and relaxing in the backyard to enjoy some of the uncommonly good September weather before reality hit and Minnesota's harsh winter began. We all knew this was strange—it could snow next week!

The children, who were between the ages of four and ten, had escaped back outdoors as soon as they had scarfed down their dinner. Usually, I would have had them return and help with the dishes, but I understood their need to release all of that energy after being forced to focus and learn all day long while the playground was beckoning them, calling their names.

Suddenly, I heard the elephant stampede that I recognized as all four of them traveling at high speed. I peered out the window above the kitchen sink and saw them all barreling toward the house, one right on the tail of the other, wide-eyed as if they were being chased. As it turned out—they were!

Parenting requires a lot of detective work. Usually, it's not very difficult. The cookies are missing, and the crumbs lead to the culprit. There's a big glob of toothpaste in the sink, but only one toothbrush is wet. (This situation also incriminates the non-toothbrushers for their lack of hygiene.) I was briefly perplexed as to what had spooked the kids so greatly.

What I didn't know was that, apparently, the kids had brilliantly invented a new pastime in which they would stand at the end of the fence, by our neighbor's yard—as to not break the rule of going beyond the fence—and throw sticks and other "tree stuff" at passing cars. I would find out later that they had a whole system going where they would take turns gathering and throwing. It was "perfect" because they were just beyond the normal sightline from the house, but we could hear them, so we figured all of their giggling was all in good—legal—fun.

This situation was brought to our attention by the large man who was angrily stomping his way through our backyard toward the house. It was a very odd sight to behold, as visitors never arrived from beyond the fence in the backyard.

The kids flew past me at the kitchen sink and disappeared loudly up the stairs with an air of terror. My husband, Dave, who had been working in the garage, intercepted the stranger in our yard and asked the man if he could help him. The gentleman was livid because his car had been struck by a flying stick. He was in an uproar about the ordeal, and he could not believe the audacity of these children. He had seen the kids, pulled over right there, and chased the kids up to the house.

Dave was shocked and he apologized profusely, saying that we would take care of the situation, but the man was not satisfied. He shook his head and grumbled in disgust as he retreated to his car parked somewhere beyond the fence. We listened as he hastily drove off.

Parenting is a big learning curve. We had never dealt with anything like this before. We sent all four kids to bed right then, almost two hours early, which was a huge deal. We'd never done that before. There were tears all around. Everyone knew they were in trouble and that they had done wrong, and we honestly didn't know how to handle the situation. We told them we would talk about it tomorrow.

After school the following day, I had all of the kids work together painting a twenty-five-foot-long sign that read "WE'RE SORRY." We all worked together to hang the sign on the outside of our fence. We left it there for a couple of days in the hopes that that man would drive past again and see their heartfelt apology.

We never heard one way or the other. Did the man drive past our fence on a regular basis and end up seeing the sign? Or was it a one-time thing, and he was just lucky enough to have encountered our well-aiming children on his only drive past? Many of our neighbors and friends in the community inquired about the sign over the next few weeks. Each time, we let the kids explain its origin to them.

It's important to teach kids that when they make mistakes (as we all do), they need to make retribution for their actions. There was no way for the kids to do that directly to the man that day, since he only stayed in our yard for a short time, but hopefully the kids learned this lesson by the way that we handled the situation. They ended up giving up their new pastime, though, because I never saw another stick on the road behind our fence.

WHAT COULD POSSIBLY GO WRONG

"Your babysitter wants to know if you're supposed to tip the fireman?"

A Slippery Situation

Lorina Stephens

E VERY PARENT COMES TO recognize that very ominous moment when silence descends in the middle of the day. That silence may as well be a space-launch Klaxon to burst your eardrums. It means DANGER! It means HERE THERE BE DRAGONS! It means OMG WHAT ARE THE KIDS DOING?!

Adrenaline is usually a parent's best friend in that situation because it allows you to move at superhero speeds, travel through walls, and use X-ray vision and hyper-hearing.

It was exactly that sort of moment that occurred on what seemed a peaceful, innocuous sort of afternoon when the children were allegedly napping. You'd expect things to be quiet. But this wasn't that sort of "the kids are napping" kind of quiet.

In full parent-alarm mode, I apparated from sofa to bathroom. I have no idea why my trajectory took me to the bathroom, but it's wise never to question instinct in such a moment. It was a surreal moment when I stood in the doorway. I wasn't quite sure what I saw seeing. There was no way . . . nuh-uh . . . what the? My naked two-year-old daughter (why is it always two-year-olds who introduce you to a stroke?) sat on the floor, quite happily and gleefully smooshing thick, gooey, concentrated pink soap through her tiny hands. In fact, there was an entire gallon of the soap all over her, the floor, the walls, the toilet, the vanity. Soap, I might note, that was at a concentration of 10:1. Soap I thought she'd never be able to access.

I do believe the first words out of my mouth were "Oh, sweetie!" followed by reaching for the bathtub taps, securing the plug, and mechanically assuring myself a bath would solve everything. Just put the child in the water and let her frolic while I mop and scrub pink goo from, well, everywhere. It would be okay.

The plan was sensible, except for the fact when I lifted her up under her arms, she just sort of slid through my hands like a squealing, greased pig. If at first you fail, try again. And fail. And try. And fail. Did I mention this was surreal? And because of that, I think my brain sort of veered off into another dimension. She held her hands up to me, wiggling soapy fingers in glee.

Returning to pragmatism, I scooped her body into my arms and set her carefully into the rising level of warm water in the tub, realizing my mistake a moment too soon. The ultra-concentrated soap on her body met the water, and an explosion of bubbles and foam erupted like some sort of slapstick cartoon. I was sure I'd slipstreamed into a kids' movie. Any moment, some flying super-duck would zoom into the scene and rescue everything.

But no. Instead, like a mythical wizard, I parted the seas (er . . . foam), made an island of that giggling child, turned off the water, and realized it would take many, many baths and rinses to get her, shall we say, squeaky clean. But the first imperative, with my daughter content in a paradise of bubbles, was to get the floor clean so I'd have somewhere to put her when at last I could dry her off. I also needed a safe place to stand so I wouldn't do a slide of my own.

I armed myself with a sponge and a bucket of water. That methodology turned out to be ridiculous because a sponge tends to just make more foam. So I grabbed a cleaning cloth. That worked. However, when the wash water in my bucket became so saturated with pink soap as to be useless, I emptied it into the kitchen sink, which produced yet another problem—because all that foam was going to take until the next century to subside down the drain.

Right. Leave the foam in the sink. Just fill the bucket with fresh water, get back to the child who might very well be drowning in bubbles, let alone water, and there you find your four-year-old son, awakened from napping by the commotion, blue eyes wide with wonder at the spectacle in the bathroom. He was reaching for the edges of his T-shirt, plainly in a move to join in this bubble extravaganza, when I plonked the bucket down, sloshing water as I did so, and pushed him back from the bathroom, plainly denying him this extraordinary fun in what he took to be parental repression. Wailing ensued. My daughter plainly agreed and set up her own harmony. I think I may have joined them in a full choral cacophony.

It was several hours later that both bathroom and daughter were de-pinked, un-gooed, and cleaner than they'd ever be again; my son assuaged; and both content with cookies and Sesame Street in the living room. And it was also the last time I ever purchased an entire gallon of concentrated soap.

THE WILD ONE

Tammy Brown

"I T'S OKAY," I REASSURED my son. "Everything's going to be okay." I gently rubbed my son's curly head and took a few deep breaths.

"Wait a minute. Where's your sister?" I asked Carson, knowing that since he had just regained consciousness, he was as clueless as I was. "Haley! Haley!"

A few minutes earlier . . .

I was on the floor playing with the kids, Carson and Haley. Diagnosed with diabetes before his second birthday, Carson dealt with a slew of challenges. We met with a diabetes specialist to learn all we needed to care for our chronically ill toddler. The educator overwhelmed us with the needed information and warned us about diabetic scenarios that might arise. As thorough as she was, however, she never warned us about how the disease might affect Carson's sibling, Haley.

Haley is twenty-two months younger than Carson, and she came out of the womb with an agenda. As soon as she learned to crawl, she was getting into everything. Things only worsened when she learned to walk, which, of course, she started at only eight months old. As the baby in the family, she demanded to be the center of all attention. If she couldn't be, then we knew she was somewhere doing something forbidden.

As we were playing on the floor, suddenly Carson passed out. Because his blood sugar was rarely within range, he would sometimes pass out when his sugar got too low. I tried to wake him up and get him to drink some juice, but he wouldn't budge. This meant that I needed to get his glucagon and give him a sugar shot.

I went into panic mode and focused my full attention on bringing Carson back to consciousness. Sometimes, what a mother sees as a crisis, a child sees as an opportunity; so was the case with Haley. Everywhere she looked, she saw adventure, and with every adventure she took, I got another grey hair.

While I was handling the crisis at hand, Haley snuck off. It wasn't until Carson came back to consciousness that I noticed she was missing.

"Haley!" I called. No response. "Haley, where are you?" More silence.

It was after the third time I called that I finally got a response, but it wasn't from Haley. Instead, our dog, Sadie, came running to my call. Trotting lightly and wagging her tail, Sadie ran up the hall to greet me. Something wasn't right. How did you get wet? Touching her slicked black hair, I realized it wasn't water—she was covered in Vaseline.

My second panic mode of the day kicked in as I recalled hearing that Vaseline could be poisonous for children if they ate it. What if Haley ate it? I ran in the direction Sadie had come and found a happy Haley rubbing herself with Vaseline. Her original canvas had run off, so she started using herself for her art.

Fortunately, at the end of the day, all was well. Carson recovered from his low blood sugar, and Haley did not ingest petroleum jelly. The dog, however, was another story. I gave her a bath every day for a week and a half before I got all the Vaseline out. When I look in the mirror and see the grey overtaking the brown in my hair, I know that a few of those grey hairs came from the time my daughter jellied the family dog.

I Swear! I Only Turned My Back for 5 Seconds!

Amilee Weaver Selfridge

I HAVE OFTEN WONDERED how many funny stories could open with phases like "I only left him/her alone for one minute!" or "I swear I only turned my back for one second!"

I've heard lots of these stories. Laughed at lots of these stories. Once I became a parent, it seemed like all I ever did was tell these kinds of stories (though the laughter did not always come as quickly as it did when the stories were about other people's kids.)

Apparently, kids don't need long to get into all sorts of trouble.

The worst part about it—knowing that fact doesn't seem to help! No matter how hard you try to be vigilant, they still find those split-second gaps and trouble always ensues.

My son is a ninja. He was born a ninja. Since day one, all it has taken is a millisecond and he can cause trouble of epic proportions.

One such story began with a simple diaper change—nothing out of the ordinary. I changed his diaper, then as I went to put his pants back on, I noticed he had my wedding ring in his hand. (How he got it off my finger without me noticing was beyond me.) In the second I looked away to finish putting on his pants, the ring was gone.

After a thorough search of both him and the floor, I began wondering if he had eaten it.

I wasn't too worried, even though it had happened before. (Don't judge.) Not with my ring, but he had eaten plenty of things he shouldn't have before. (Okay, I lied. Judge all you want.)

Back to that moment though—I wasn't too worried. After past experiences, I knew what to watch for in case the ring was stuck or unable to pass through his system.

Again—kids don't need long to get into much trouble. And my little ninja was fast.

I continued to watch him while still moving forward with my day. While working on my computer later, the oven beeped, pre-heated for dinner. I walked over to put our food in the oven and walked back, and—in my defense, it really had been less than five seconds—he had taken the L key off my computer keyboard and put it in his mouth.

I tried to grab it before he could swallow it, but . . . ninja.

Down it went.

This time, I was worried.

He became uncomfortable. Started grabbing at his throat and was struggling to swallow.

Luckily, his breathing was still okay.

My husband chose this opportune time to walk in the door from work.

He quickly came to my son's side and asked what happened.

Loud coughing spared me from needing to answer. My son coughed for a few more seconds, then pop!—out flew the L key and my wedding ring!

My husband's head swung toward me. With a knowing look, he laughed. "Really? Your ring? And whose keyboard is that from?"

"In my defense, I swear I only turned my back for five se—"

My response was cut off as my husband dove toward my son, grabbing my ring that was already back in his mouth.

Seriously, you can't take your eyes off kids for even one second. Trouble, I tell you.

The First Day Accident

Don Drewniak

M Y DRIVER'S LICENSE WAS in my wallet two days after my sixteenth birthday. Yes, I passed the Massachusetts driver's test, but events would soon prove I shouldn't have. My father owned a 1954 light green, four-door Ford. He also had access to a job-related pickup truck.

When I showed him my new license that evening, he made the mistake of tossing me the car keys and saying, "Take the car tomorrow." I called two of my best friends, Lenny and Jack, to tell them I would drive them to school.

We made it to Durfee High without anything resembling an incident. But on the way home, traveling too fast downhill on the lower stretch of Columbia Street, I came too close to a parked car. Bam! My right-rear fender hit the protruding end of a wrap-around bumper. Bumper 1—fender 0.

Except for racing at drag strips, seat belts were all but unknown in the fifties, so it's no surprise we weren't wearing them. I slammed on the brakes and screeched to a stop. Thud! Jack, who was in the front passenger seat, smacked his head on the interior of the windshield. No damage to the windshield. No permanent damage to his head.

"Shoot!" yelled Lenny as he slammed into the back of the front seat.

"Any damage to the other car?" I screamed.

Lenny uttered a less-than-convincing "no" a few seconds later.

I shifted into first and left a few feet of rubber as I rapidly departed the scene of the crime. Not a word was said as I headed toward my house. Parking the car just out of sight of the back of the house, I told the other two to stay in the car.

I assessed the damage—a shallow dent ten inches in diameter. Racing into the yard, I opened the cellar door and grabbed two ballpeen hammers from the Old Man's workbench. (It was commonplace in the 1950s, at least in my hometown of Fall River, to refer to one's father as "the Old Man.")

Off we went to a secluded area near a deserted mill located less than a mile from the house. We jacked up the right-rear of the car and removed the tire. I went to work. Lying under the fender, I held one hammer against the outside of the dent and began gently tapping the inside with the other one.

This was something I learned to do a few years earlier from having watched the Old Man when he owned an automobile repair shop.

Several hundred taps later (or so it seemed), music came to my ears from one of my co-conspirators: "It looks like new."

With my face, arms, and shirt covered with five years' worth of gunk that had fallen on me from underneath the car, I slid out from under the fender and let out a whoop. It looked perfect to me. But how would it look to the Old Man's eagle eyes? After a week went by without him saying anything about the car, I finally began to sleep soundly.

I secured a part-time job at H. Schwartz and Sons Lumber and Hardware shortly after the accident. A few weeks later, I bought my first car, a 1952 Ford, for $99.00.

"Wait a minute," said the Old Man as he inspected my new pride and joy. He then headed to the basement of our home.

He returned a minute later with the two ballpeen hammers. "Here," he said with a slight smirk, "these are in case you put a dent in your right-rear fender."

A Birthday Egg

Sarah Das Gupta

WHEN MY FIRST DAUGHTER, Mistha, was born, I was living in Kolkata, India, with my husband, a newspaper journalist. Mistha had begun to talk at ten months, and by her first birthday, she was fluent in English and Bengali. She understood the importance of birthdays and, above all, their connection with presents. On November 6, she was very excited from five o'clock on, when she insisted on getting up and waking the rest of the household with her.

By breakfast time, she had already changed into her party dress of peach-colored silk, adorned with white lace, and matching sandals.

I should perhaps mention that Indian houses are not always suited to young children, especially when they first learn to walk. The floors are stone or even marble, which makes them slippery and rather hard to land on if you should fall. Mistha had the habit of running at speed much of the time. This had led to several rather painful experiences.

We had also made the stupid mistake of buying a fashionable coffee table with a glass top cut in a curved shape. In Kolkata, people would often pick a design from a London or New York furniture store, and the very talented local carpenters would copy it. Usually, the copy was so accurate and well-made that a customer would be hard put to see the difference. Often, furniture is transported by workmen simply carrying it from one part of the city to the other. We had enjoyed watching our new tables, beds, and chairs progressing through the city streets and seeing the men have their lunch sitting at our table and an afternoon siesta on our beds on the pavements and at the junctions en route!

This had all been enjoyable until Mistha was born. By the time her first birthday arrived, she already had scabs on both knees and had banged her head on the kitchen door!

After lunch, she was very excited, trying to play with all her presents at the same time. Suddenly we heard a loud scream followed by agonized sobbing. We both rushed into the front room.

Mistha had fallen over onto the wretched glass table. She was lying on the floor in floods of tears. It took several minutes to realize what had happened. We discovered eventually that she had tripped and banged her head very hard on the curve of the glass top of the table. Fortunately, the glass had not shattered, which would have been catastrophic. As it was, the bump on the left side of her head was already as big as a chicken's egg and in the process of becoming a delicate shade of blue and yellow.

By the time we had pacified her with chocolate buttons, the bump had changed to a darkish blue goose egg and the elegant peach-colored dress had dark smears of chocolate over the front.

We were worried because the lump was still expanding. It was a Sunday afternoon, and the doctors we knew lived on the other side of the city. We had one neighbor who was an orthopedic consultant and a very well-known surgeon. My husband said, "I'm sure Dr. Saha wouldn't mind having a look at her. Any doctor should be able to assess whether she needs an X-ray or further treatment."

I agreed, so he went off to find a rickshaw. Soon Mistha was sitting up in the vehicle with an ostrich egg on her head. It was really spectacular by now, with dark blue at the edge, pale blue in the center, with crisscrossing yellow stripes.

"Daddy, I can sort of see the bump on my head if I twist round like this and close one eye."

At this point, her father caught her just before she fell out of the rickshaw.

"I'd sit still if I were you," he said. "I don't want to haul you out of the gutter. You don't want to break the egg."

"Is it really an egg?"

"Don't start her off on that idea," I chimed in. "She'll be wanting to check what you're saying."

They returned about an hour later, just as I was about to panic that something serious had occurred. I saw Mistha sitting triumphantly in the rickshaw with a large bag of sweets. The egg had changed to a very dark blue and the yellow streaks were turning green. She was talking to the rickshaw wallah. Apparently, she told him to not be as silly as her parents and never buy a glass-top coffee table. What he understood from that would be difficult to assess.

Dr. Saha said the bump would gradually go down but that we should watch to make sure she didn't become drowsy. The peach dress was never quite the same.

Before she went to sleep that night, Mistha asked if you could have two birthdays a year. I think you can imagine the answer!

Multitasking Blues

Devin A. Reese

As I raced to finish grading my students' papers online, I offhandedly noticed the subtle action in the background. While I read and scored essays on environmental conflict, my two-year-old son kept crossing back and forth, in and out of the playroom, without so much as a "Hi, Mommy!" sent my way. No matter. Gus wasn't fussing for attention, which gave me time to get my work done before we had to pick up his brother from preschool.

Some of the papers were so poorly written that I didn't spend much time on them. But several were skillfully crafted to show how conflict arose over natural resources after periods of unusual scarcity, like droughts or floods. I put those aside to read more deeply and decide which level of A they merited. It was always refreshing to find a handful of papers that were excellent.

There Gus was again, toddling behind me and up the stairs, presumably to his room. The house still smelled like paint after my adventure to brighten up the playroom walls with a lemony yellow. I got up to turn on the overhead fan and then noticed on the kitchen clock how little time I had left to finish the grading. In forty-five minutes, we needed to pull out in the car toward Beverly Preschool.

"Concentrate," I commanded myself as I pored over the last few essays and etched point values in the margins. One of them seemed oddly professorial for an online student, so I snagged a paragraph out and pasted it into Google Scholar. Sure enough, plagiarized. I'd have to email the dean of students about it for potential disciplinary action. Plagiarism was, unfortunately, all too common in my class of adult learners.

"Gus, we need to leave in ten minutes!" I shouted as I started entering the other grades and feedback into the digital gradebook. An essay by a return-to-college mother was particularly evocative, describing how tensions over oil supplies stoked up the Iraq War. Hers might be the one A+ on this round, I thought as I punched the last grade into the form and hit Submit. "Gus, let's go."

Shoot—we were going to be late. He wasn't in the playroom, so I bolted up the stairs. His room door was closed and locked. Knock, knock, knock. "C'mon, sweetie, it's time to go get your brother." I heard the door unlatch and I pushed it open.

Gus was standing in the middle of his small room with a pleased smile. In my hurried state, it took me a moment to focus on the situation at hand. His clothes were marked with brush strokes of blue paint. Wait . . . he had seen me painting the playroom. Uh-oh.

His walls were splattered with blue dots and drips, some of them marking the rug below. Oh no, this must be the finger paint we kept downstairs in the art cart. His bed sheets still had little red and black rockets, but they now surrounded a liquid lake of blue in the middle of the sheets.

Gus proudly announced, "Mommy, look! I painted my room blue."

Kyle's Homemade Conditioner and Moisturizer

Sarah Mallari Bucu

H AVE YOU EVER USED mayonnaise on your hair to see if it's an effective conditioner?

I haven't.

But my daughter, Kyle, sure has—when she was three years old.

It was one of those busy days when I thought I deserved a thirty-minute nap. Kyle and I just had our lunch, and after reading her a short story, I thought that would be enough for her to nap as well.

How wrong I was.

I was already in dreamland when I heard a loud thud. I immediately stood up to check on Kyle, but I was totally unprepared for what I saw.

Kyle's hair was covered in mayonnaise, her hands clasped and covered in the condiment. She was smiling, unfazed that I had just caught her in the act of exploring her new discovery.

I wanted to cry in frustration, but I decided to just clean her mess by giving her a shower. As I was about to reach her, I felt something sticky as I stepped on our wooden floor. When I checked my foot, I found that there was coffee all over the floor. I tried my best not to scream and asked Kyle what was she thinking.

"I wanted to know what the floor would look like with coffee on it," she replied nonchalantly.

I closed my eyes in frustration, deciding to clean my daughter first and take care of the slimy floor after. And as much as I hated mayonnaise, I did my best to bathe my slimy daughter while con-trolling my anger.

After what seemed like an eternity, our wooden floor was again clean and sans the odor of mayonnaise. I thought I deserved some dessert after all the scrubbing that I did. As I looked for the ingre-dients, my mother's instincts told me that something was wrong, especially since the leftover cream in the fridge was missing.

Then I saw Kyle with her face, arms, and legs slathered with cream.

She just smiled, showing me her dimples, and said, "Moisturizer, Mommy."

A Quick Nap

Tammy Brown

I KNEW I SHOULDN'T do it, but I had an overwhelming urge to close my eyes for just a second. I was at home with my two children who were only two and four years old at the time, too young to be left unsupervised.

But I had the flu, and I felt awful. My goal was just to get through my mandatory parental duties; I simply had to keep my children safe and fed and then hope to feel better the following day.

I put Nickelodeon on the television and found a spot on the couch. My eyes slowly closed, but I snapped out of it and held them open wide. I can't go to sleep. I simply can't. The children are way too young to fend for themselves. My internal pep talk helped for a minute or two, but I soon found myself fighting to stay awake again and then giving myself the exact same speech.

The kids noticed nothing of my struggle. They had several of their favorite toys spread throughout the living room, and they took turns between playing and watching a cartoon. They were happy, and they were silent, neither of which helped me stay awake.

Eventually I gave in. I'm not sure how long I napped, but I awoke with a jolt.

Oh, no! This is awful. What a neglectful mother!

Through foggy eyes, I looked around the room. The children seemed to be doing exactly what they were doing before I lost my sleep battle. There was a different show on television, but everything else looked the same.

I rubbed my eyes and took a deep breath. I got lucky that time, and I wondered if they even noticed that I fell asleep. I got my answer as I studied the scene a little more closely.

It was summer, and I had fallen asleep in a T-shirt and shorts, which gave my little artists lots of skin surface for their masterpiece. Everywhere that skin was exposed, there was either a sticker or a drawing in marker. They had apparently entertained themselves by decorating their mother.

I had no energy—the flu had drained every bit of it—but I somehow got up from the couch and made it to the bathroom. I looked in the mirror to see that my face hadn't been off-limits. There were various doodles on my forehead, cheeks, and nose.

I erased my children's artwork while they continued to play with their toys and watch a show, and they didn't even respond to their mom's new look. I had simply been one of the toys they used for entertainment, and once they ran out of canvas, they moved on to other things.

I didn't find humor in the scenario at the time simply because the event only gave me an extra chore as I scrubbed and de-stickered. However, when I look back, that day has become a fond memory. And I have to say that getting a nap that day was totally worth the extra cleanup!

Is This a Phase? Or is This Going to Last Forever?

"Two happy meals and an anxious meal

First Day, Worst?

Joyce Frohn

M Y PARENTS DIDN'T REALIZE that the first day of parenting me would set the pattern for all the rest.

First of all, they weren't planning on a second child so soon. Like so many mothers in the sixties, my mother was told that nursing was birth control. She should have known better given that her mother's children were all about eighteen months apart.

They were generally happy about it and started planning. They had a written birth plan; my father was going to cut the cord like he had for my older brother, and an aunt promised to come and help with housework.

The only problem my mother had was trying to figure what that large lump under her rib cage was.

Her doctor never said. He was a large man in most ways, but as all his fans said, he had "lovely small hands."

When she felt labor pains beginning at about three o'clock, she called the hospital. The nurses said she should come in; it would be hours before birth, but it would be good to be there.

So my mom called my dad at the church (where he was an assistant pastor) and called my aunt in, and my parents calmly drove to the clinic for a quick check. As my father was filling out the insurance form, my mother had barely settled into a chair when her water broke. Two nurses rushed over, helped her into a wheelchair, and rushed off. One of them said over her shoulder, "She'll be in the prep room at the hospital."

As my father tried to remember such difficult things as "When is your wife's birthday?" and "Where do you work?" my mom was being wheeled across the street to the hospital and her doctor was being paged. She went to the prep room where, back then, women in labor were first shaved and then given an enema.

My mother got her clothes off and moved from the wheelchair to the exam table. The nurses patted her hand and assured her that they would get the labor room ready. So there she was, with her feet in the stirrups and wearing a paper sheet, when a young nurse came in with the enema, the shaving cream, and the razor.

The nurse lifted the sheet and dropped everything she was carrying. She ran out of the room whimpering. Things started happening fast.

A bunch of nurses came running in with a gurney and rushed my mother into the delivery room. Her doctor finally got there. He was panting so hard that my mother kindly offered him the oxygen mask the nurses were giving her. She couldn't understand why he was so pale. To her, this labor was easier and much faster than her first.

It seemed the doctor had hardly seated himself when he started urging her to push. There was a faint cry, and then he was lifting up a baby—me. My mom realized that the head was toward her. Suddenly, everything made sense. The baby was a footling breech. Nurses rushed to put me in an incubator.

My mother glared at her doctor. He patted her hand. "I had it all planned," he assured her. "I was getting your room ready for the C-section. I didn't want to scare you." She kept glaring as she realized that lump under her rib cage had been my head.

My father didn't locate her until she was in a hospital room. It was the fourth room he'd run into; luckily, he hadn't blundered into someone else's birth. "Where's the baby?" he blurted out.

A nurse finally came in with a pink, wrapped bundle. Unlike the calm blue bundle he had been handed less than two years ago, this one was moving. I was described as looking like "someone trying to escape a straitjacket." I only calmed in my mother's arms.

"What took so long?" my mom asked.

The nurse frowned. "We had to trim her nails. She scratched three nurses."

Apparently, I went through the rest of my childhood choosing the hard way, fighting back and trying to hit the ground running.

THE BLIND PRESCHOOLER

Tammy Brown

I ALWAYS LOOKED FORWARD to picking my daughter up from preschool. Not only did it mean that I would be able to reunite with my youngest child, but I always loved the stories she told about the events of the morning. As soon as I would ask if she had fun, I would get a complete, detailed play-by-play of what happened, who wasn't a good listener, what everyone was wearing, and so on. Honestly, Haley could give more details than the most skilled reporter.

One day when I picked her up, however, my normally garrulous child was quiet, so I began an interrogation process to find out why she wasn't herself. Her reluctance to give me information had me worried that something bad had happened, so even though I could tell Haley had had a bad day, my questions continued. Yet her response to most of my questions was a grunt, a huff, and then the crossing of arms.

Eventually, I did give up, since I theorized that someone who loved to talk as much as her wouldn't be able to hold out forever. This hypothesis turned out to be correct, and after several hours back at home, Haley finally approached me with something she felt important to share.

"Andy's eyes have gone bad!" she finally said in an emphatic voice.

The comment caught me off guard because I didn't quite understand how a classmate's eyesight could make my preschooler come home in such a bad mood.

"Okay," I responded, "What do you think is wrong with them?"

"I don't know. I just know he can't see anymore."

My concern shifted from my daughter's welfare to the health of one of her favorite playmates.

"Can you tell me a little more? If he's really having trouble with his vision, Haley, I probably need to call his mom so she can take him to the doctor."

Haley's terse response was simply "Yeah. His eyes aren't working."

"Okay, sweetie. I'll give his mom a call, but could you tell me a little more so I can share that information with her? How do you know that his eyes aren't working?"

Little hands found their place on little hips as she explained. "I know because he used to tell me I was pretty all the time, but he doesn't anymore."

Somewhat relieved but still thinking there must be more to the story, I again probed.

"Okay. So Andy doesn't tell you that you're pretty anymore. But is there any other reason you think he has bad eyesight?"

With a hint of frustration in her voice, she responded, "No, mom. That's it. He used to be my boyfriend, but I had to dump him because of his eyesight. Boyfriends are supposed to say you're pretty."

It took maximum effort to hold back my laughter, and I didn't end up making that phone call to Andy's mom. Haley had a bad day, but I learned something very important. My youngest child wasn't going to be a pushover, and I would never have to worry about her giving her affection to a boy who didn't appreciate it.

The Piñata

Dave Bachmann

I WAS DRIVING 678 miles so I could deliver a bright green papier-mâché dinosaur to my son who just went off to college. I know that sounds a little crazy, but by the time Teddy had packed his 1999 Toyota Corolla with all his clothes, books, and hockey gear, there simply wasn't room for the dinosaur.

Or at least that's what he told me.

I thought about flying to Madison, Wisconsin, with the dinosaur but was told I would have to buy him his own seat. So I figured driving would be cheaper. And possibly less embarrassing.

It wasn't.

I was only twenty miles from home when I got pulled over by the State Patrol. After producing my license, I respectfully asked, "Was I speeding, officer?"

Without answering, the officer motioned to the green dinosaur I had strapped into the passenger seat and asked, "What's up with that?"

"I'm taking it to Madison. To my son. He's starting college."

"Uh-huh," the officer mumbled, clearly unimpressed with my backstory. "I don't suppose you're planning on trying to drive in the HOV lane with that thing sitting next to you."

"Oh, my . . . no, officer. Wouldn't consider it."

"Well, I've seen plenty of others try it." At this, he paused before asking, "You been drinking?"

"Just tea, officer. Nothing more."

"Okay, well, be on your way. And think about tossing Dino there in the backseat so you don't get stopped again."

I thanked the officer and continued on my way.

The dinosaur had been around for a long time. I bought him for Teddy's fifth birthday party. It was to be the day's main event. I would tie a rope around his waist, hoist him four or five feet into the air, blindfold the kids, and let them whack at the dinosaur until he broke apart and spilled his sweet, colorful contents all over the ground.

Teddy, however, had other ideas.

"We can't hit Danny," Teddy quietly informed me, midway through the grilling of the hamburgers.

"Who's Danny?"

"Danny is the dinosaur. He doesn't want us to hit him."

"And how do you know this?"

"He told me."

Placing a gentle hand on Teddy's shoulder, I calmly pointed out that dinosaurs couldn't talk, particularly ones made of papier-mâché.

"You don't need words to know when someone loves you," Teddy quietly remarked.

And from that moment on, Danny the Dinosaur became a rescue dinosaur.

I stopped mid-afternoon at the Middle-of-Nowhere Diner, which clearly lived up to its name. No one in the parking lot. Good. The sun was beating down mercilessly, and there was no way I was going to leave a papier-mâché dinosaur in a hot car.

I sidled up to the lunch counter and placed my order, carefully propping Danny up on the stool next to mine. The waitress, who looked like she had been waitressing since biblical days, eyed me suspiciously.

"What about him?" she grumped.

"Just some twigs and seeds," I joked, to no one's amusement other than my own.

The waitress shrugged and disappeared. The sounds of hushed whispers and giggling from the kitchen soon followed.

As Danny and I waited, our solitude was abruptly interrupted by a gaggle of road workers who burst into the diner and piled into two booths behind us. Their animated voices trailed off as they became aware of the presence of a middle-aged man at the lunch counter and his bright green dinosaur. More hushed voices and giggling.

Great.

The waitress reappeared with my cheeseburger and fries (no twigs or seeds) and shuffled over to the road workers to take their orders. Perhaps it was because my expectations were so low that the cheeseburger tasted so good. No matter. Things were looking up.

And that's when the waitress reappeared.

"Courtesy of the gentlemen," she remarked dryly, motioning to the road workers, whereupon she set down a huge platter in front of Danny with a single, enormous rib bone.

The road workers erupted in laughter.

I smiled weakly, quickly finished my cheeseburger, nodded my thanks to the road workers who were still rollicking with laughter, and slunk back to my car, Danny in tow.

My wife and I mistakenly thought that as Teddy grew older, he would lose interest in Danny. But he didn't. To the contrary, Danny became a fixture at Teddy's hockey games where he was quickly adopted as an unofficial mascot. Through elementary school, middle school, and finally high school, Teddy and Danny were inseparable.

Which is why I was making the ten-hour trek to the University of Wisconsin to deliver a green papier-mâché dinosaur to Teddy's dorm room.

I arrived around dinner time, hungry but anxious to make my delivery. I had a map of the campus that Teddy had received with his admission to the college, and in short order, I was standing at his dorm room door.

It was then that I experienced sudden reservations about this whole thing. This was my son's new life, and I was intruding upon it—with a green papier-mâché dinosaur, no less. Maybe Teddy had meant to leave Danny behind. Maybe he just didn't know how to tell me that it was time to move on. Maybe . . .

I was about to retreat to my car and reassess the situation when the door opened. Teddy was on his way out and nearly careened into me.

"Dad!" he exclaimed. And just like that, he threw his massive arms around me and Danny the Dinosaur, smothering us in his embrace. We both started to cry.

No words were spoken. Because none were necessary. As the five-year-old version of Teddy had so innocently put it, "You don't need words to know when someone loves you."

THE CHRISTMAS SURPRISE

Amilee Weaver Selfridge

W E ALL KNOW THAT one of the best parts of Christmas is the surprises! Gifts from your loved ones that you never expected.

When my family arrived home from spending Christmas Eve and Christmas morning with extended family to find our furnace no longer working, it wasn't quite the surprise I was hoping for.

Lucky for us, some unfortunate technicians were on call at a local heating company and could come help us out.

A new furnace was required.

Somehow, though—a Christmas miracle, most likely—we could actually have the broken furnace replaced that day!

As the technicians were putting in the replacement, I heard a shocked call for us to bring any buckets or bins we might have, right away. Not really what you want to hear . . . especially on a Christmas evening when you just purchased a new furnace. My husband rushed to help as I tried to keep the kids away without exploding from the anxiety of the unknown.

When my husband walked back into the room carrying two bins, followed by one of the technicians also carrying two bins, I was shocked to find that it wasn't actually an unpleasant surprise. The bins were full of balls, cars, and toys!

What on earth?

The technician explained that when he opened a panel that divides the furnace from the rest of the system, the balls and toys began flowing out. He quickly addressed my confusion by explaining that any items placed inside vents throughout the house could end up there.

This truly was a Christmas miracle! I was gifted the knowledge of where all my kids' missing toys kept going!

Yes, that meant my kids had been loading our vents with probably more than I wanted to know (which, on inspection, was proven quite true). But their toys were back and maybe, just maybe, I could keep them from getting put in there again (which, unfortunately, was proven not true).

The best surprise of all . . .

My kids were so excited to see so many of their toys again! They thought we were giving them more gifts for Christmas.

And while I didn't plan for my Christmas to include a broken furnace, hidden troves of toys, and a hefty bill, I couldn't help but laugh. Because if parenting has taught me anything, it's that the best gifts are often the ones you never see coming—like your child jumping up and down in joy, declaring it the best Christmas ever. All because they thought you bought them their favorite toy again . . . when really, it had just rolled out of the furnace.

Parent Vs. Cellphone

Mark Daponte

T HERE WAS A TIME in the twentieth century when hearing a parent beg "Can you please get off the phone so I can use it?" meant his or her child was (actually) talking on a phone and hogging up the lone landline so much that when another call finally came through, a voice would remark, "What is going on? I've been trying to call you for the last two hours! Was your phone off the hook or . . . wait. You have a teenage kid. Say goodbye to your phone for the next few years."

In these twenty-first century times, imploring a teenage son to put down a phone is like trying to take a bone away from a hungry pit bull whose only trick is rolling his eyes in the presence of "know-nothing-and-not-hip-and-so-prehistoric" adults. Worse, a pit bull boy only barks when he's hungry: "Hey, Dad. Is dinner ever going to be ready? And no offense, but how come there's never any ice cream, oatmeal cookies, or sliced turkey in this house? The cupboards are always bare and . . . oh, sorry. My bad. I ate all the turkey, oatmeal cookies, and ice cream last night."

Yes, preadults spend more time looking at glass than a goldfish in a fishbowl, with both sharing the same wide-eyed, glazed stare. The only difference is that a goldfish moves around and moves its mouth more in one day than some sedentary teenagers do in a week.

I once strongly advised my son to give his phone a well-deserved rest for one hour. He squawked back, "It's not a phone in a phone's sense. It's a pocket TV too—which I bet you'd watch constantly too if you were my age because you once said your TV was your best babysitter, didn't you?"

I admitted that this is true and offered, "My grandpa used to say, 'Son, when I was your age, I had to only walk nine miles to school.' Now, I have to confess my hardship to you. Son, when I was your age, my TV only had nine channels . . . and they weren't on twenty-four hours a day. They all showed test patterns at 4 a.m.!"

"Whew. How did you exist? Huh . . . what's a test pattern?"

Before he ignored me for the rest of the day, I made him laugh after I said, "And when I was a kid, we didn't hang a metal coat hanger on the TV's indoor antenna to get better reception. We couldn't even afford metal coat hangers, so we used the wooden kind. Nice try changing the subject, kid, but you still have to put your phone down for an hour. Starting now."

We bargained, bickered, and argued over how much time he and his best inanimate friend should not see each other. I admit it—he wore me down. A phoneless hour became fifty minutes, then forty-five minutes, and finally, a half hour.

In a further effort to have a conversation and something in common, I say, "We both love Batman, right? I mean, any Batman is great. 'The Batman,' a Batman, the cartoon Batman—doesn't matter as long as it's Batman, right? So how about we see real old-school Batman? For your no-phone half hour, let's stream on our TV this guy named Adam West instead of you listening to that guy named Kanye West on your phone."

My DNA match and I watched Adam and his sidekick drop villains instead of swear words. Moreover, whenever the two crime fighters answered a "Bat Signal" from Commissioner Gordon, they didn't rush to a club with hundred-dollar bills to throw but wound up wildly throwing punches—which widely missed scores of "villainous" stuntmen/henchmen. We couldn't decide what was more painful for Batman and Robin: taking an errant punch to the body or having to wear skin-tight undies. My son and I temporarily bonded for twenty minutes and found that the goofy show held up rather well. And my son finally didn't hold up his cell phone to his face for a solid thirty minutes. After the show was over, he showed me a sent group text message:

"Hey. My real old man just turned me on to this real old-school Batman. You gotta check it out! And Dad. One last argument. How come it's okay to watch this show on your big TV screen but not okay that I watch it on my tiny cell phone screen?"

Reading Aloud

Ed Meek

"READ TO YOUR KIDS" is a mantra drummed into parents today, and it really seems to have sunk in. Books aimed at the young continue to be a growing market for publishers. As you know, the *Harry Potter* books were an international best-selling phenomenon that brought riches both to publisher and author. For parents, it is no longer enough to take books out of the library; we need to own *Goodnight Moon* and *Where the Wild Things Are* so we can read them over and over again to our enthralled children. It feels good to buy a few books for a child's birthday rather than running up the charge card with plastic toys.

Now, the reason to read books to your kids is to foster a love of reading. The idea is that if we read to them, they will be so enamored with the experience that they will go on to become great readers themselves. The subtext of the story is that this love of reading will also hopefully erect an intellectual barrier of literacy that will protect the young from the evil Cyclops television. Although television doesn't exactly eat the young in the same way Cyclops ate Odysseus's men, television certainly seems to command their attention. Moreover, television stifles the imagination, which as we all know is a quiet room in the brain where a child goes when he or she reads or is read to by a loving adult.

Now, it just so happens that my wife and I love to read. "A room without books is like a body without a soul," said Cicero. Our house is full of books. The idea of reading to children appeals to both of us. For the past twelve years, in fact, with few exceptions, either I or my wife has read for a half hour to an hour each night to our son. We started with board books and rhyming books, fantasies and myths and nursery rhymes, from the brilliant and disturbing Maurice Sendak and the Brothers Grimm (whose cautionary tales no longer quite make sense) to the obnoxious Dr. Seuss and the benign Shel Silverstein. As our son got older, we met the ill-mannered yet entertaining Rotten Ralph, witnessed plastic cowboys and Native Americans come to life before us, and spent a couple of weeks in a wonderful secret garden. We read all the Oz books, including a couple not so Oz written by someone other than Frank Baum. We read, reread, and read again—on request—the entire *Narnia Chronicles* (all seven books) by C. S. Lewis. We slogged through Brian Jacques' violent rat adventure books. We loved getting to know Harry Potter, Huckleberry Finn, and Alice. Lately, we've moved into young adult literature (a fuzzy category). We recently read *To Kill A Mockingbird*, *The Catcher in the Rye*, and *The Great Gatsby*.

And what is the result of these years of reading aloud? Has our twelve-year-old turned into a great reader? Someone who always carries a book with him just in case he has a few minutes to read while waiting in line? Someone who likes to curl up on the couch in front of the fire with a classic? Someone who asks for books for his birthday? Alack, alas, no. The result of all this reading is that our son loves to be read to. He loves to listen to books on tape when we take long trips in the car. He enjoys hearing Maureen Dowd read to him on Sunday mornings. He does not especially like to read by himself. In the summer, we require that he do a little reading each day and he puts it off until he's in bed. He reads for fifteen minutes and then falls asleep. We've given him subscriptions to *Muse* and *Skateboarding*, but he seems not so much to read them as to just look at the photos and read the captions. He did read *Harry Potter and the Goblet of Fire*, a genuine accomplishment at 729 pages, but that was because we were taking a trip to Corsica and had to spend a lot of time waiting in airports.

In other words, it was a fluke.

Yes, he has succumbed to the Cyclops in the den. He prefers watching television to reading. He loves the X Games with their competitions in skateboarding, snowboarding, and trick biking, all nature shows, and the History Channel. But he is not really discriminating. Given the chance, he will watch whatever is on. After television, he reaches for skateboarding, snowboarding, or car-racing video games.

Was all of our reading then nothing but a waste of time? Well, no—because my wife, my son, and I have all enjoyed it. I hadn't even read a lot of those books. My wife had read most of them, but she enjoyed reading them again. Reading aloud is an activity that brings us back to our childhood, making us feel young again and bringing back the pleasure of reading great books and hearing them read aloud. As many adults have discovered, there's a lot of great writing aimed at kids. Reading aloud reminds us why we like to read. Nightly reading has also become for us a family ritual. It lends structure and uniqueness to our family life. It's a family activity that we value. My son has benefited in a couple of unexpected ways too. At school, he does well in English in both reading and writing, and his teachers always comment that he has a wide range of knowledge.

Until the invention of the printing press, and for a long time after that, when books were read, they were read aloud. At school and at home, entire sections of books were memorized. There's a distinct pleasure that comes from reading aloud and from hearing a well-written book read aloud. It's different from reading silently. Books like *The Great Gatsby* work better read aloud than read silently. Lines like the following beg to be read aloud: "So we beat on, boats against the current, borne back ceaselessly into the past."

Not that we have given up on the original objective. We imagine that any day now, our son will tire of video games. He will shut off the television and banish the Cyclops to the world of darkness. He will take a book down from the bookcase, lie down on the couch, and begin to read. He will lose track of time, so engrossed will he be. As he reaches the end of the book, he will wish it could continue. "Well," he'll say, "I can always read it again."

We expect this to happen right around the time he starts eating his vegetables.

A Moment

Tony Daly

There's a snowball on the floor.
Its name is "Baby," and
it's getting bigger all the time.

It started with a bad night's sleep,
then a missed nap and a lot of yelling.
"Let go!"
"Get down!"
"Don't hit your brother!"
"Don't! You'll break it!"

Then my savior arises,
in all her sleep-deprived glory.
She looks as well as I feel, but
"Tag—you're it!"

While I enjoy a few seconds with my tea,
and fear my return to the ring,
When the wrathful goddess roars,
it makes me feel more sane,
if only for a moment,
if only for a moment.

A Sharp Idea

Tammy Brown

I parked the car, gathered my bags, and walked toward the house, ready to relax after a long shift at work. As soon as I put my hand on the knob, the door opened and my daughter greeted me in a panic.

"Mom, I totally forgot to tell you about our band concert!"

I didn't understand the need for distress, so I calmly replied, "That's okay. When is it?"

"Tonight!"

I started to understand Haley's angst at that point, but I still tried to be a calming agent.

"Take a deep breath. It'll all be okay. What time does it start?"

"The concert is at 6:30, but I have to be there by 6:00."

"Oh my! We better get ready then. It's already 5:30."

"Mom, you don't understand. I can't get ready. She said that we *have* to have black pants, and I don't have any!"

As more and more of the situation came to light, I became more and more frustrated, although I tried not to let it show.

"Come on. Let's look through your closet and dresser. I'm sure we can find something that'll work."

Together, we walked into Haley's room and began looking. I couldn't even find a pair of dark blue pants to use as a substitute. Finally, at the bottom of one of her drawers, I found an old pair of black pants.

I held the find up and asked, "What about these?"

Haley looked hopeful for a fraction of a second, then her face quickly drooped. "I remember those. I stopped wearing them because they have a big hole in the knee."

"Try them on. Maybe it won't be that noticeable."

Haley did as she was told and then modeled the pants for me. Just as she had said, on her left knee was a hole about the size of a grapefruit.

"Mom! What am I going to do? Mrs. H will kill me if I show up in these."

I looked around the room for anything that might give me idea. Indeed, her situation wasn't looking good.

"Wait a minute, Haley. I think I have it."

I grabbed a black Sharpie from her desk. "Come here."

Haley came closer, and I went to work coloring her knee while she protested.

"This is never going to work," she said. "I can't believe you're doing this."

When I was done, Haley looked in the mirror.

"Hmm. I guess it will work," Haley sadly replied.

"It's going to have to work. We have to be there in ten minutes. Besides, it will hardly be noticeable on stage."

We arrived at the school right at 6:00. Haley dashed into the school band room while I found a seat in the auditorium. The band came on stage at 6:30, and from where I was sitting, Haley looked like she was wearing a regular pair of black pants.

On the way back home, Haley said that no one even seemed to notice her knee.

"I'm glad," I replied, "but I really need you to tell me about upcoming events sooner."

"Don't worry, I will. Besides, I don't know what color pants might be required next time, and the only color of Sharpie we have is black," she said with a laugh.

"Good point. Now let's get you home and into the bath! You have some serious scrubbing to do!"

SAY WHAT?!

"My toddler just discovered the word 'Why'."

INNOCENT UNDERSTANDING

Jesse Neve

O UR BIG LITTLE CROWD huddled into the funeral home that chilly winter night. We were there for my cousin Donnie's visitation. Our kids were two, four, six, and eight, and they hadn't known my cousin, but they had been to funerals before and understood why we were there.

We visited with some other relatives briefly, and then we filed through the somber lines and spent some time looking at the nice display of photos from his lifetime. I didn't know Donnie that well either—my mom had eleven siblings, so many of my cousins were much older than I was. So it was nice to see the pictures of him as a son, an uncle, a brother, and a dad and to learn more about his life.

The kids were interested in the photos and were able to pick out some relatives that they recognized. Daniel, age four, saw a picture of Donnie at a young age holding up a dead deer that he had proudly shot while hunting. In full sincerity, he looked up at me and said, in complete understanding, "Oh. Is that how he died? The deer shot back?"

THE NAME CHANGE

Nan McKernon

W HEN SHE WAS IN fifth grade, my ten-year-old daughter blabbed to everyone at her elementary school, and even a few families in the neighborhood, that the man I intended to marry was a registered sex offender.

Only he wasn't.

She simply didn't want to share her mother, whom she'd had to herself for several years following the divorce from her dad. Crafty as she was, she figured this was the best way to make this gent disappear, and for good. This is not a tale of a mother in denial unwilling to overlook her daughter's trauma for her own selfish desires. It's a story of a tenacious, intelligent, and willful girl whose sole source of security was the mother she would safeguard at all costs.

Her name is Alexandra. We call her Lex.

Lex had experienced deep abandonment by two important men in her life and was, as a result, deeply distrustful of all men. It was nothing untoward; it was an issue of unreliability. I was advised to create some stability for her, so I dug in hard in the consistency department. By third grade, she'd come to depend on Mom as her prime source of self-esteem, entertainment, and companionship. We were like Maverick and Goose, without the tragic ending, or Ethel and Lucy without the chocolate assembly line; we were each other's everything. So when I met a man who would become my other kind of everything, not only did it not go over well, but a lesser man would have run from the endurance challenge Lex set in his path.

It was a Tough Mudder—the stepdad course.

I waited nearly a year before introducing Lex, then almost ten, and her older brother, Jake, to Mac, a childless divorcé who was retired from over two decades in Special Operations with the United States Air Force and working as a first responder with a local ambulance company. He was calm, introverted, and played Dungeons and Dragons in high school. We were polar opposites, and the balance and love we shared was unlike anything either of us had ever experienced.

Lex hated him on sight.

"He's bald," she said the night they'd first met. "And ugly. And I'm never going to like him." With that, she closed her bedroom door, opened a years-long silent treatment, and started the rumor that is now legendary fodder at dinner parties.

Lex has an older brother seven years her senior, so she has many only-child traits (as attested by me, an only child): She likes to be in control, and it can be challenging for her to adapt. At ten years old, when newcomer Mac challenged the only stability Lex had known for years, it had to be devastating, no matter how much dedicated solo time with Mom she still had or how much reassurance she was given; life as she knew it was changing.

Mac and I anticipated a difficult transition and sought professional guidance. The advice was seemingly simple: Mac needed to stay consistent in his efforts and show up for her no matter how much Lex resisted. She was testing him, and it could take time. Lots of time. If he backed off, he would prove her beliefs accurate that all men were unreliable.

No pressure or anything.

So he showed up for her. Three days a week, while I was student teaching at a local college, he made sure she got on the bus safely; she called him a pervert who wanted to ogle young girls in short skirts. He attended every softball game to cheer her on; she said only biological parents were allowed to attend games. When he asked for her blessing and help choosing an engagement ring, she refused: "My mom doesn't like rings."

Around this time, I noticed that Lex stopped getting invitations to her friends' houses for play dates, and many were refusing our invitations as well. Knowing adolescent girl friendships could be tumultuous, I reached out to a close friend, who was the mother of Lex's closest friend.

"I heard about Olivia's birthday on Saturday and realized Lex wasn't included. I hope she didn't do something, given how close they've become this year. Do you know anything?" I asked.

"Well, I think . . . well," she hesitated. "I think Lorraine is afraid you'll bring, well . . ." she stuttered.

"Come out with it, Ella. What's going on?"

"Well, it's the thing with Mac and . . . the registry . . ."

I was baffled. What registry? Our wedding registry? We didn't register for anything. It was the second marriage for us both. We didn't need anything. "What on earth are you talking about?" I asked.

"You know, Mac and the sex offender thing. I'm sure you can understand why parents are concerned. I mean, no judgment or anything. I told Bob maybe it was one of those 'he was eighteen and she was seventeen' kind of deals," she offered.

"The *what*?!" I practically shouted. "Mac and what sex offender thing? Ella, what on earth are you talking about?"

"Lex told Abby that Mac was on the sex offender list. She told all the girls at lunch. She told Maureen in the office that she wasn't allowed to go home alone with him."

"Oh. My. Gosh. Ella, Mac isn't a sex offender! For goodness sake, do you honestly think I would *marry* a sex offender? Why didn't you ask me about this? Oh my goodness, I have to figure out what to do. I'll call you later, but do me a favor, *please*. Start

94

telling everyone that Mac is *not* a sex offender. Will you do that for me please?"

"Of course. Yes. Gosh, Nan. I'm so sorry!"

"I can't believe this. Someday, maybe, we will laugh about this, right? Maybe?"

And someday did come. The therapist was right. It took time—years, in fact. A lesser man would've given up, but Mac kept showing up for Lex who is worth showing up for. Their picture hangs on the wall of her middle school—him in his dress blues, for military family day, the signup for which was just left out on the kitchen counter, filled out in her loopy handwriting. He sat at the table night after night troubleshooting math problems with her despite her unwillingness to look him in the eye, learned to braid her hair using YouTube when Mom was teaching morning college classes, walked her to the gate for her first flight overseas, taught her to change the oil on her first car, and helped her choose her prom dress.

In January 2021, when Lex was seventeen, she approached me with a request I gladly obliged. On Father's Day of that same year, Mac opened the result of that request: a legal decree.

She'd petitioned the court, a minor needing parental permission, to modify her legal name. She'd legally added the surname of the man she once refused to acknowledge, the man she once told everyone was a registered sex offender. Because not only had he shown up for her. He had stayed.

Integrity

Viji K. Chary

I WAS SURPRISED TO find that my five-year-old son, Rishi, had an unbelievable sense of integrity.

One evening, my brother-in-law was playing games with Rishi. When I told Rishi that it was his bedtime, he said he still wanted to play. So I gave him five more minutes. When the time was up, Rishi put away his toys without a word and was ready to accompany me upstairs.

My brother-in-law was dumbfounded. He had never seen a child willingly going to bed when he was having fun.

"When Rishi agrees to something, he sticks to it," I told him.

But integrity comes in different forms.

In the upstairs bathroom, a wicker hamper sits next to the toilet that Rishi uses. Rishi had a bad habit of picking at the wicker, leaving it ratty. We repeatedly told him not to pick at the hamper.

One day, my husband passed by the bathroom while Rishi was on the toilet. Through his peripheral vision, he saw Rishi picking at the hamper.

My husband came back to the bathroom and asked Rishi, "Were you picking at the hamper?"

Caught by surprise, Rishi was silent. My husband repeated his question. Moments passed as Rishi carefully thought.

Finally, he answered. "I won't answer that question."

Our five-year-old had just pleaded the fifth!

You Fell For That?

Amilee Weaver Selfridge

M Y STORY BEGINS DURING the dark ages. You know, *that* dark time—the one with the masks, the sourdough craze, and everyone trying not to murder their family during "quality time."

Well, my family's "quality time" had been going on for six months at this point. As a family full of medical conditions and lacking practically any immunity, we had the opportunity to stay quarantined well past the initial two weeks of isolation.

In fact, the next school year had started, and we had the privilege of having our oldest son attend school virtually instead of in person. Which meant I *also* had the privilege of virtually attending first grade. (Hip hip hooray.)

A few months into the school year, my son and I happily (overstatement) sat down at our computer to start our school day. We had survived (also an overstatement) until Friday. It was almost the weekend.

The teacher was greeting the children over video chat. She asked them what time they had each woken up. Children began giving their responses.

"8:00 a.m."

"7:30 a.m."

"7:45 a.m."

Bouncing with excitement, my son unmuted the computer for his turn. "3:30 a.m.! Mom, I won! I won! I slept the fastest of all the kids!"

Though his excitement was as contagious as the dreaded virus, I still couldn't dredge up any excitement of my own.

That's what happens when you spend 47 hours with your children before breakfast even begins. Not to mention that had been happening for about 6,000 days straight now.

Luckily, my son didn't notice my grimace as he went on and on in praise of his win.

Just a few more hours. I could handle that.

A few hours passed, complete with reading, writing, math, and a dance party in lieu of gym.

We had done it. There were only a few minutes left in class, and then we could say we had survived another week.

At the close of the class, the teacher made an announcement to the kids, which left me far more excited than my son's earlier announcement. She was pregnant! She explained how she had a baby growing in her tummy.

Instantly, my son started asking questions about how the baby got in the tummy. He also shared some graphic, though luckily inaccurate, thoughts on how the baby comes out of the tummy.

Anxiety spiking, I jumped to the computer to make sure he was on mute, almost fainting with relief when I saw we were indeed muted.

The teacher thanked the kids and began her end-of-class speech, my son still spouting off ideas of how he thought babies get both in and out of the stomach.

I told him he needed to listen to the last minute, then he could talk about it again after.

I stood up and began walking away. I was halfway across the room when I heard it—his teacher calling on him.

I spun around to see him with one hand raised, the other hand unmuting his computer.

Oh my gosh! He was going to tell his teacher all his ideas about the baby since I wouldn't listen! But it's not just her—it's a class of twenty-five kids. All these kids are on computers. Most are in a room with their family as well. My son cannot share his graphic thoughts with all these people. We can't traumatize children like that.

I geared up to sprint over as fast as possible to save others (and myself, let's be honest) from the mortification of what was coming.

No, no, no. This can't happen.

I pushed on my back foot, ready to take off. To fly.

My foot pushed straight into a rug, which crumpled with the force of my trajectory, and I flew!

Straight down.

Straight into the floor.

Face-first.

With a crunch.

In that same second, my son's voice rang out, unmuted for the world to hear . . .

"Hi!"

Hi? Did he just say hi?

Yes. Four hours into the day, while the teacher prepared to end the class, with excited chatter in the air from her announcement a minute before, my son raised his hand and said . . .

Hi.

I wiped the blood dripping from my recently crushed nose and decided then and there that it would not be COVID that would kill us. We wouldn't survive long enough for it to have a chance. That I was sure of.

The Death of a Pet

Robert Runté

WHEN MY DAUGHTERS WERE eight and two, we had to put down our fifteen-year-old dog, Portia.

Portia had suddenly yelped in pain one evening, and I had taken her to the vet after hours. The vet diagnosed a pancreatic attack, gave her painkillers, and sent us home but had me bring Portia back the next morning for tests. By that afternoon, they had found a very large tumor in her pancreas and, as tactfully as possible, told us that the prognosis was not good. The vet explained that dogs will routinely conceal health problems from the rest of the pack as long as they're able, so there was really nothing to be done by that point. Nevertheless, we had held out some hope that with pain medication and a controlled diet, Portia might enjoy some quality of life for at least a few months.

It was not to be. It quickly became obvious, particularly at night, that Portia was suffering terribly. With pain medication, she would rally for an hour or two each day to bounce around in public like her old self, but then she would tire, curl up in a ball, and spend the rest of the day whimpering. I made the decision to have her put down sooner rather than later, and my wife reluctantly agreed it was time.

Telling Tigana, our oldest, was difficult, but she was already a kid who didn't want things sugarcoated. So my wife explained that we were going to have to help end Portia's life because she was suffering. We resisted the temptation of saying things like she was being "put to sleep" or, as one of our friends did with their younger child, say that we had sent her to "live on a farm." Tigana was tearful but brave and accepted that it was for the best.

Telling Kasia, our youngest, was going to be a different matter since we weren't sure how much a two-year-old could understand. We were still debating the best approach when Tigana took the matter out of our hands.

As Tigana and I picked Kasia up from day care, the following dialogue was exchanged in the back seat:

Tigana: "You know Portia was sick?"

Kasia: "Portia sick?"

Tigana: "Very sick."

Kasia: "Portia very sick?"

Tigana: "So they decided to kill her."

Kasia: "They *killed* Portia?"

Tigana: "She was sick, so they had to kill her."

Kasia: "They *killed* Portia?!"

Tigana: "She was sick, so they killed her."

Did I mention that Kasia had a bad cold that day and that she had just learned to say "sick" when she felt unwell and wanted medicine? That she had in fact been saying "I sick" all that day because she wanted to stay home rather than go to daycare, but that we had taken her in anyway in order to deal with Portia?

Naturally, when I arrived home with Kasia, the first thing my wife asked her (in a depressed-about-Portia-tone, at that) was "How are you, Kasia? Are you still feeling sick?"

"No!" Kasia shouted, trying to suppress her coughs. "Not sick!"

Cola

Steve Denehan

My daughter wrote a story
and read it to me
the guts of it was this
there was a lady
who was in love with two men
and the men loved her back
she couldn't choose between them
but luckily for her
and for them
she was a scientist
and a mad one at that
she invented a machine
the two men stepped inside
there was a flash of light
a loud sizzle
and lots of smoke

When the smoke cleared the two men
were one
she couldn't believe it
they couldn't believe it
they celebrated with a delicious meal
the thing was

one of the men loved Pepsi
but was allergic to Coke
and the other loved Coke
but was allergic to Pepsi
the waiter brought a tall glass
cola, ice-cold
the two men
as one
took a swig
their death was instant

My daughter closed her notebook
asked me if I liked her story
I told her that I did
she asked me what the moral of the story was
"Don't drink Pepsi?"
"No!"
"Don't drink Coke?"
"You're being silly, Dad!"
I thought for a while

a long while
a ray of sunshine landed on the carpet
"I'm going outside!"
she announced and was gone
taking the moral of the story with her

4 Shots + 1 Needle = a Surprise

Annette L. Brown

mom·my guilt
/mä-mē gilt/
noun informal North American
the culpability moms feel ten to twenty times a day due to
having done something wrong, nearly wrong, or very wrong
(even if the mistake is made in the name of sanity)

Dr. Reynolds clicks his pen closed. "Cole is behind on two
shots and has two upcoming. He needs four shots." What? I
missed his last vaccinations? Instant mommy guilt. "He can
have all four today—along with his blood drawn so we can
check on his anemia," Dr. Reynolds adds casually as he snaps
his clipboard closed.

I grimace. My stomach churns. "Four? Won't that make him
sick or something?"

"He'll be fine." The doctor's raised brows indicate he wants
an answer—now.

I watch Cole, who sits cross-legged on the floor, leaning over
a wooden puzzle. He isn't listening. I weigh the options: two
vaccinations today and two more next week, or four today and
done. I wiggle my fingers, recalling the drive here—clutching the
steering wheel, knuckles white, leaning forward. It's a three-town,
hour-plus trek of afternoon traffic. Ugh. A glimpse of my reflec-
tion in the small mirror by the door reveals crazed eyes and frazzled

hair, rather like a brunette Cruella de Vil. "Okay. Do it." Ouch. Pinch of mommy guilt right in the soft spot under the bicep.

I explain the four-shot plan to Cole, emphasizing that only a brave kid can have four shots in one day (more guilt for lying). His eyes widen into blue saucers—"Um . . ."—and then scrunch with doubt. "Okay."

When the nurse brings in the four syringes, Cole's lips press into a thin line. A lower-lip quiver follows the first puncture. Trembling lips and quiet tears follow the second. By the fourth shot, he's bawling. I want to join him, create a chorus. I refrain, reminding myself I'm the grownup. Guilt twists my stomach because I approved the four shots, and more because I know we're not finished with needles.

I pull Cole onto my lap and hug him until he's calm. His cheeks burn pink. He pants, lower lip in pout-pose.

"I'm proud of you. You're so brave." He rests his head against my chest. I kiss his blond curls, try to gather the courage to break the news of the final needle. I'm fully engaged in self-loathing when the nurse pokes her head through the door and chirps, "They're ready for you."

"Thank you." I decide to tell him when we get to the lab. Only three doors down. I love procrastination.

When we turn into the lab, Cole goes rigid and tightens his grip on my hand. He glares at me with eyes of steel. "Mom," he says through gritted teeth, "are they taking your blood today?"

Yikes. He remembers the lab. "No, honey," I squeak, mommy guilt nearly strangling me. "Um . . . remember, we came here today because your blood is sick and—"

Cole doesn't wait for me to finish. He does not cry out. He invests all his energy into pulling away, feet flailing, torso wriggling. I lift him, press him to my chest. Hands on each of my shoulders, he arches and uses anger-strength to push away. I keep to the room's borders, edge toward the reception desk.

A young male nurse and a seasoned female nurse look up in unison. The woman states, "This must be Cole. Come around the desk. We'll have him sit right over here."

I offer a crooked smile and inch toward the chair, a mass of flying limbs slowing my pace.

"Oh my, he's strong. Mrs. Brown, if you'd just hold him."

He's serious about escape. I don't blame him. I want to escape.

"Come here! Help us!" the veteran female nurse calls to the younger male.

"Here, you take that leg—ouch!—and I'll . . ."

"Oh, just hold—maybe right here—"

"Okay, I've got him—no, no, not so much, I'll just—"

"Let me get his arms," I finally suggest. "You take his legs." I wrestle his arms down.

The male nurse grabs both his legs. The female takes one of his arms to get started. Finally, Cole gives in and stops struggling. He pants. When she punctures his skin with the needle, he doesn't move. He watches the blood pooling in the vial at the same rate his eyes increase in size. He scowls, then looks up to the ceiling and shouts, "I hate my family! I want to live alone!" The young male nurse and I both jerk, looking first at Cole's face and then at one another. I should feel serious mommy guilt, but I burst out laughing, and so does the nurse.

The scene just strikes me as funny. Here we are, three adults tussling with this four-year-old—who is nearly winning and who ultimately resolves to divorce the lot of us, his whole family, even his dad and big brother who are innocent of the entire ordeal.

When the nurse unties the rubber tourniquet, Cole slides from his seat, crosses his arms, and tucks his fists into his armpits. He squeezes his eyes into his "mean look," then angles his back toward me and marches toward the exit. I follow at a safe distance.

I unlock the truck. "I'm sorry you want to live alone."

Silence.

"I'll miss reading stories to you every night, especially your favorite, *The Knight and the Dragon*."

Silence.

Cole climbs into his car seat, tilts his chin up and away from me. I buckle his seatbelt.

"Your dad and brother are going to be sad." I slide into the driver's seat. "Your brother's going to have to sleep alone now."

He catches me spying on him in the rearview mirror and yanks his head toward the passing landscape.

"I think I'll go get some ice cream at Baskin Robbins."

Silence.

"Would you like some?"

"I want to live alone," Cole mutters again. I sneak a peek in the rearview mirror. Fists buried in his armpits, pout firmly in place, blond curls tussled, cheeks still flushed from the ordeal—he really is darling.

"I understand. I made a mistake telling the doctor that four shots plus drawing blood was okay today. I'll miss you." We drive in silence the rest of the way. He deserves a break. "I know you don't want ice cream. I just need you to come in while I get mine."

Silence. But he shoots furtive looks my way.

As we walk toward Baskin Robbins, he struggles between maintaining the raised-chin, back-toward-me pout and sneaking glances. Ice cream crushes resolve.

"You can get ice cream," I tell him casually. "It doesn't mean you have to live with us."

"Okay. But I still want to live alone."

Ice cream in hand, we settle onto a bench just outside the store and sit in silence, both enjoying our favorite flavors. I scrape the bottom of my paper bowl. "I wish you'd give us another chance."

He trains his eyes on his ice cream, slowly licks his spoon. He looks like he is seriously trying to decide whether he wants to live with us. Finally, he speaks up. "Okay. But I never want to have four shots again!"

"That's fair. I'll try my best!"

As we leave the parking lot, I smile at Cole through the rearview mirror. He's finally shed the pout. I also check my stomach for any mommy guilt—just a little lingering behind the pralines and cream.

Today's decision was about convenience—and realism. I walk a tightrope, balancing career, kids, husband, house. Sometimes, despite the mommy guilt, I have to make decisions that hurt for a bit, like four shots might, but that ultimately get the job done—like four shots did.

Staying Focused

Jesse Neve

W E HAD ALL FILED into the front pew that Sunday morning. We always picked the front because then there was less to look at and "we" were more likely to pay attention.

Today we were on time, everyone was dressed, and everything was good. I looked down the row to my husband, Dave, and smiled. He was holding one-year-old Ben, and between us sat the rest of our crew: seven-year-old Sarah, five-year-old Jonathan, and three-year-old Daniel.

It was a peaceful day at church, which was not always the case. Everyone was sitting quietly, (presumably) listening to the priest and singing along with the well-known songs.

Right in the middle of the sermon, Daniel tapped my leg and motioned that he had something to whisper to me. Of course, I was pleased that he had a comment on the priest's thought-provoking words. I leaned down and Daniel quietly said, "Mom, have you ever run anyone's underwear up a flagpole?"

So much for everyone paying attention in church.

Visiting Time

Fiona M. Jones

M Y CHILDREN WERE THE ones who didn't throw public tantrums. Followed me like ducklings. Ate their vegetables. Went to sleep at night like contented little lambs.

Perhaps it was luck, or a natural docility on their part, or maybe my clever little parenting hacks that stood me in good stead. Maybe that time-consuming nightly sequence of warm milk combined with bedtime stories followed by cozy quilts in a cold bedroom that's supposed to pay generous dividends in "me time" after 8:30 p.m.?

I'm not so sure that would have worked on its own. No, the real hack was this: that I and/or Daddy would "visit" the children about half an hour after their bedtime. I would walk in, talk softly, rub their backs if they were still awake, then quietly leave, job done. They wouldn't bother getting out of bed before I came, because they knew I was coming. By the time I made my visit, they were too relaxed and sleepy to want to get out. And on the rare occasions when I forgot to visit them, they very usefully assumed I'd come in after they'd fallen asleep.

My husband and I took our undisturbed evenings almost for granted. It was only when staying overnight with friends that we discovered not all young children stay put after bedtime. Some of them get out of bed repeatedly and pretend they're thirsty, or hot, or cold, or afraid of the dark, or disturbed by the noise of the TV.

I always wondered—silently, of course—whether a little "visiting" might have made everyone happier.

As my sons reached school age, they began to immortalize their favorite routines in pictures and stories. One of them drew me standing by the bunk bed exchanging speech bubbles with him while his younger brother lay snoring. One of them was asked to write a little descriptive piece about his parents.

"I love my Mummy," he wrote, "because she visits me."

You know how teachers are always vigilant for indications of an irregular home life? My son's perfectly innocent story made it look as though he had two absent parents who only saw him occasionally. It left the teachers wondering who he actually lived with, and whether this arrangement was supervised by social services . . .

Which goes to show that whatever you do as a parent—even if it's entirely normal—it will somehow turn around and bite you in the derriere.

GOAL: KEEP TINY HUMANS ALIVE

"How does she do it without help?"

WHITE WATER CANYON KIDS

Gail Collette

T HE BRIGHT COLORS, LIGHTS, and sounds of laughing beckoned our family into the Wonderland, even though the outrageous prices at the ticket/bracelet booth were daunting.

My hubby and I sought out rides for our three children and niece. Their ages ranged from five months to nine years. We happily passed by the gravity-defying roller coasters and the screams that came from the free-falling and blast-off rides.

After the merry-go-round and kiddy airplanes, we were glad to find a boat-type ride for the whole family.

Of course, the line was long on the hot day. I carried five-month-old Abby in my pouch-like baby carrier. She went through her bottle while Angela (age nine), Tim (age five), and Tessa (age two) went through all the sips and little snacks we had brought. I wiped their sticky, sweaty faces and hands.

I was tempted to use a wet cloth to also wipe the smirk off the face of the dismissive teen who was operating the ride. The sturdy white-water raft with six upright seats was ready for us, and three of the kids got on, but the young man didn't want me to take baby Abby on the ride. There was no signage with that rule. I insisted that Abby would be perfectly fine strapped to me in the carrier.

I looked to see how my husband, Alvin, was doing with the kids on the raft and saw instead that he was standing behind me. Three shocked little faces looked back at me from the spinning and bobbing raft that was then set adrift.

I spared one second to flare my nostrils at the teen staff member who had loaded the three kids on the raft and sent them into the rapids without an adult.

Angela looked like she wanted to grab onto her section of the solid round wheel at the center of the raft seats. Instead, she helped the little ones feel safe. She gripped the wheel with preschool Tim on one side and toddler Tessa on the other. With her hands over their tiny ones, Angela kept telling the younger ones that she would help them hold on tight.

Within seconds, I was running along the treed shoreline to follow the quickly moving raft. The three voyageurs tipped up and then back on the large raft. To them, it was an extreme sport. My baby onboard the carrier gurgled with a broad smile as I ran. My husband puffed behind.

I caught a glimpse of the raft as a large wave swept over the youngsters. We exchanged helpless glances as they sped by on their way into a dark cave opening. I could only yell, "Hold on! It'll be okay!"

Exhausted, I arrived at the off-ramp a few minutes after the little ones. They were soaking wet and shivering in the hot sun. I tried to hug all three, but two-year-old Tessa stood aside with her chin out and shoulders rounded. She shook a water-wrinkled finger at me and said, "Don't you ever do that again!"

The Influenza Diaries

Katie Sakanai

M Y CHILDREN REALIZED WHAT I was up to when I pulled into the spot at the doctor's office. The six-year-old knew first, of course. The crying passed in a wave from older sister to younger. The cold November rain mimicked their tears as we walked from the car to the office.

We pass well-adjusted young children in the hall. They are composed. One asks my eldest, "Are you getting your flu shot?" and she answers a sober yes. The mom says she's taking him out for french fries now, and I say cheerfully, "See you at Good Times!"

We arrive at the doctor's office. Scores of young children are sitting and quietly playing. My youngest and I read three or four books during the wait, but every now and then, a whimper escapes. My eldest tries to befriend all the kids in the waiting area and find out if they too are being subjected to this torture. After her tour, she comes back to me and says, "All these kids are getting flu shots!" I tell her this is a flu shot clinic. The doctor's office is open after hours, and the poor nurse has to stab child after child with preventative medicine. The front desk assistant looks exhausted as though she's been here since 7 a.m.

The children my daughter befriended are called back. She hears a loud "owie" emanating from the ominous shut door down the hallway. She draws my attention to it. I point out the fact that it was brief-lived. The children emerge unscathed. Both holding their stuffed animals, they take too much time choosing their stickers, and that annoys the mom. Be grateful, I think.

My children are called back, but incorrectly. No one can pronounce their names because I have given them old-lady names. This probably has already negatively predisposed us to the nurse. She wonders what mom gives unpronounceable names to her girls. But no matter, the true test is still to come.

The children begin to cry as we walk into the room. The six-year-old wants the three-year-old to be the guinea pig, but I tell her, "Big kids go first." The nurse gives her a choice of arm or leg to give some semblance of control, which she is about to lose. She chooses leg, but it's like the scene in Indiana Jones and the Lost Crusade as we pull down her jeans and I hold her down. The nurse asks me to make sure I have a good grip on her arms. It's already over, but she continues to cry a bit, as she will for the next few hours, hopping on one foot and earning a Golden Globe nomination for best actress.

The true test of my parenting is yet to come. The little one is screaming and fighting. She is doing the toddler thing that makes them impossible to hold on to. I think this must be a vestige of an earlier time—the prey turns its bones into jelly in order to wriggle free from the predator's grasp. She seeps, melts to the floor like a puddle, and loses a shoe. The smart little one crawls under a chair where I find it nearly impossible to reach her. She's shouting, "I want the flu! I want the flu!" With a few more attempts at jelly-bones, she is finally wrangled to the table. She is kicking, so the nurse is now clearly ticked off at the risk to her own welfare. I cover the child like I imagine an octopus consumes a crab, using every appendage I've got.

The shot is long since over, but the resentment and anger will last until the ice cream hits lips. The nurse exits quickly without a look back. I encourage us to get the heck out of there, but the toddler needs to find her lost shoe. She's sitting on the floor, repeating

"That was terrible!" I tell her it's time for ice cream, but she must make sure I know that "THAT WAS TERRIBLE."

No one meets my eye as we enter the full waiting room except for a teenager who's willing to give me a smile. She has not yet learned to judge other parents cruelly and unfairly. After all, just two days before, I modeled complete calm and composure as I got my own flu shot. We walk to the sad sticker station—who are these characters anyway? Not a recognizable princess in the bunch—where taking too long is the least of my worries. The older one chooses a sticker halfway through the roll, ripping off a long line like she's won at the arcade and annoying the tired front-desk lady. The little one doesn't want a sticker. She is too offended.

I carry her to the car and use all my whole-brain-child parenting techniques, but there's no chapter on flu shots so they're completely ineffective. We drive straight to Good Times in the cold rain. The toddler is screaming and I finally lose it, telling her I can't drive in the dark while being aurally assaulted (because of course it's daylight savings time and pitch black at 5:45). And did I mention the cold November rain? Why can't her three-year-old brain jump ahead one mile to the part where I buy her ice cream? Older sister tells her to quiet down so I don't miss my turn. She's more practical that way and knows I have a track record for missing turns.

We're in the drive-through. The order is placed. I'm unsure if this was worth it. I'm considering immunizations for only the most terrible-sounding diseases and just taking our chances with influenza. Will our good health and sanity be preserved and restored? Only time and frozen custard will tell.

Always a Surprise

Amilee Weaver Selfridge

IT WAS THE AFTERNOON of my birthday when I received the best birthday surprise I could have ever asked for. I was going to be a mom!

It was a true surprise.

You see, a few years earlier, my husband and I learned we could not have children on our own. Since then, we had spent the years trudging through the adoption process. We had just switched a couple of weeks earlier to a new adoption agency after having gone through a couple of failed adoptions and *so* much time waiting.

As I sat on the couch waiting for my husband to return home so we could celebrate, I received an email from our adoption case manager. A prospective birth mother had picked us, and the baby would be born in just a couple of months.

We were excited to meet the prospective mother the next week. But within a few minutes of being together, I noticed something: The baby *never* stopped moving in her stomach.

I had been around plenty of pregnant women before—several sisters, friends, and coworkers. I had even seen their babies kick and move. But never had I seen a baby move *constantly*.

Throughout the entire meeting, her stomach was like the ocean, waves flowing back and forth. Only these waves were little feet and hands trying to press their way out.

This little boy never stopped.

We met her a couple more times before the birth of our oldest son. And each time we met, it was hard not to stare at her dancing belly.

Once our son joined our family, we were surprised (though we shouldn't have been!) that he still always needed to be moving. As a baby, that meant constantly being rocked, walked, or in a swing. And as he grew, he was way ahead of schedule when it came to crawling, walking, and running. He was always on the move, even in his sleep. Once he was a toddler, he could easily climb out of his crib. But he moved so much in his sleep that we still kept him in the crib; otherwise, he would fall straight off his bed.

One day, I heard him wake up from a nap in his crib. As soon as I heard him, I knew I had to rush to get him out so that he wouldn't climb out on his own. The moment I opened the door, he stood up on the frame of the crib and jumped!

I ran to catch him, but I was too far away. He landed with one hand extended, supporting all his weight.

At first, it didn't seem too bad—he cried for a moment and then quickly moved on with his day. But I kept an eye on him over the next couple of hours. Though still playing around like normal, he kept looking at his wrist where he had landed. He wouldn't let me look at it or check it out. My gut told me something was wrong, and I decided to take him to the doctor.

As we sat in the waiting room, my son was all over the place. No one would ever guess he was hurt. The doctor was going to think I was crazy to bring him in.

I wasn't wrong about that.

Right as my son was doing a handstand, the doctor came in. As I explained my concerns about his wrist, the doctor kept looking between my son and me, trying to hide his disbelief.

My son wouldn't let the doctor examine his wrist either, so he ordered an X-ray to "rule out a break." It was most likely just bruised and tender, or at most sprained.

After ten tries to get a picture of my wiggly boy's arm, the X-ray was done.

Again, we waited in the room for the doctor to return. This time, I stared at my son in disbelief as he ran, jumped, and climbed around the room. *What was I thinking? He really is fine. What a waste of all our time.*

As my son grabbed the doorknob to escape from confinement, I overheard the doctor and nurses talking.

"I can't believe it! It really *is* broken!"

"You owe me ten bucks!"

Not only had my son actually broken his wrist, but he had broken it in two different places.

Now, did that slow him down? Nope. Not a bit. He would still move and move.

Always a surprise.

ONE THING AFTER ANOTHER

Sarah Walker

W HILE PREGNANT, EVERY BREATH could feel strained, even after the simplest exercise. My feet would throb just from walking to the mailbox and back. During my first pregnancy, I could rest as often as I wanted. The second time around was tougher because I had a toddler to keep up with.

Thankfully, I wasn't without help—usually. My parents lived in the same neighborhood and could babysit often. My husband was also great at taking over some of the parenting duties after work and during weekends. But things weren't always easy.

I was screwed when the "crud" spread through my family. I termed it that because I wasn't sure what else to call it. We knew it wasn't COVID because we had tested negative. My daughter and I had caught it first but recovered quickly. As for my husband, it hit hard. The day he showed symptoms, I called my mom to see if she could watch my daughter so I could take care of him. Of course, when it rains, it pours. She had the crud too along with my dad. The realization clicked.

I was alone.

The laundry was in a huge pile because I couldn't physically transfer the wet clothes from the washing machine to the dryer, my belly being a basketball-sized obstacle. I needed a stool and, ironically, I was too short to reach it at the top of the hallway closet. (I freely admit that the placement of the object wasn't well thought through . . .)

121

On top of everything, my doctor had also given me the task of collecting my urine for twenty-four hours. I had to contain my golden waste in a jug that was kept in the refrigerator. So gross.

While everyone else was sick, I had to function as a single parent through their illnesses—a pregnant single parent. Demands for Tussin were high, with requests from both my husband and my folks. As the only healthy one, I had my hands full. To top it off, my toddler needed milk. A trip to the grocery store was necessary.

I was an anxious driver and socially awkward, so this wasn't ideal. I tended to search for remote jobs because I preferred to avoid human interaction. My husband usually did the shopping. Still, I did what I had to do. I pushed my daughter in a cart up and down aisles, my feet aching as I realized flip-flops had been a bad idea. There were occasional comments about my size.

"You look like you're about to pop!"

Gee, thanks. I have three more months to go . . .

When someone asked if I was pregnant, I thought about answering no just to mess with their heads. No, don't, I thought. Hold your tongue. Smile and be polite.

My knuckles were white on the wheel, baby kicking furiously in my tummy, while I drove home with the groceries. I had been holding my bladder during the entire trip, waiting to unload into my jug. I brought in the groceries, out of breath from each journey from the car to the house.

Not wanting to drive again, I walked my daughter in her stroller to our community park. She was content with her bottle of milk, but I failed to realize how hot it would be outside. I guess my brain was foggy because I had somehow forgotten that this was mid-afternoon in the middle of a scorching summer in the southeastern corner of the United States.

I was wearing those dang flip-flops again because my sneakers no longer fit my swollen feet. Each step sounded squishy with sweat. The air smelled like freshly mowed grass as I traversed through our suburb. Wind chimes on balconies were dead silent—no breeze to provide relief. By the time we were almost to the park, I regretted leaving the house. But I couldn't turn back now if I wanted to avoid a tantrum.

When we arrived, there was an altercation between two adults. I didn't know exactly what the argument was about, but it looked heated. One woman shoved a man as she yelled a list of profanities at him. I heard the meek voice of a bystander murmuring "This is a kids' playground," but her words were unnoticed by the two adults set on murdering each other. I guessed the summer heat could drive people crazy.

Nope. Nope. Nope. I turned the stroller around and sped back home. Not dealing with that.

My toddler screamed all the way home. I understood where she was coming from. She couldn't rationalize that I was pulling her away from an awkward situation. To her, I'd simply shown her a glimpse of the park and then pulled her away before she had a chance to play.

My neighbors flashed judging glances in my direction as she wailed—hence why I wasn't a people person.

Vigilant Grandma

Erika Hoffman

I KNOW IT'S HARD having babies. Although vaguely, I remember giving birth to four. But I'll tell you what else is hard—when your daughter has her first kid and you become not only chief bottle washer but also the main whipping boy as you care for her and her bundle of joy.

I didn't have a C-section with any of mine, so I couldn't commiserate with Heather on that. I don't know what it's like to have your head above the fray and beyond the curtain at your chest as you hear the freshly minted intern, right out of med school, being instructed by the ob-gyn about sewing you up.

"Never do it that way!" you hear your doctor caution. "No! You don't want to cut over there!"

"That's a bleeder!" another voice says.

Then when the baby is pulled out and propelled toward your arms, you, in a drugged state, almost swat the bloody mess away.

No, I don't know what that's like.

Back in the day (and I mean the eighties), the Lamaze technique was the rage. And yes, I fell for the pitch. I had all-natural childbirth sans epidermal, and yes, I breastfed—although my mom who had her kids in the 1950s warned me against it, saying I'd end up looking like an old, saggy dog with teats dragging on the ground. (Thanks, Mom, for that visual.)

I swore I'd be more of a help to my daughter than my mom had been to me. It wasn't her fault. My mom got sick and couldn't help other than give advice, whereas I have my health and most of my mind.

Heather wanted to spend the first month with us in our spacious house rather than in a cramped apartment while her husband worked night and day in a fellowship many states away. Of course, I agreed to it. After all, this was my daughter's first kid. My sons' babies were tended to by their maternal grandmas. I wasn't around at their actual births. This time, I was needed for the baby and to nurse my daughter back to health. I'd be a big help. I'd be appreciated. Oh, that was the intended dream scenario!

My son-in-law Moe had planned to be here for the first two weeks, although he did have to make a quick up-and-back flight to Boston. Other than those twenty-four hours gone, he was an enormous help.

The other day, he was talking about having his name changed. He wanted to shorten it to sound less Arabic and more American, now that he was an American citizen. Watching my daughter order him around, I told him I had the perfect name for him: "Step-n-Fetch."

He repeated it in his deep, accented voice, looking quizzical, not totally comprehending it at first. Then he smiled.

"And I have a surname for you too," I stated. "Not-Fast-Enough."

Because he'd gone to Boston on day five of his son's life, I drove my daughter to her pediatric appointment and her appointment with her lactation specialist.

I had nursed all of mine without any instructions. That said, I didn't think it was bad she was getting counsel—she was sore, after all, and this lady would give some tips. The lactation specialist wasn't very old, and she didn't seem like she had a lot of firsthand experience, but I guess the most important part was that my daughter was willing to listen to her advice—unlike mine!

Anyway, this lady was kind and supportive of my daughter, but . . . this lactation "pro" had these dang long, chunky fingernails—acrylic—and a blocky French manicure. And every time she grabbed the baby, my heart sank as I saw those claws near his eyes.

When we finally got back into the car, I told Heather I liked the pediatrician and that the lactation nurse was kind, but most of what they said was common sense. Then I added, "Why do they permit her to have nails like that when she's handling young infants?"

"I can't believe you!" my daughter scolded.

"What?"

"You were audibly gasping every time she held him or put her hands anywhere near his face."

"I was?"

"Yes. She rolled her eyes at me—twice!"

I thought for a moment about my daughter's rebuke, and then I replied, "Good. I'm glad she noted my concern. That way, she was extra careful with our kid!"

At dinner later, after I picked up Moe from the airport, he asked how the appointment went. I told my tale. Then Heather told him how ridiculous I was. I could tell Moe felt the same as I did. But I didn't put Step-n-Fetch on the spot or on the chopping block. Instead, I turned to Silent Sam—my husband.

"What do you think?" I asked him.

He said simply, "A nurse should have short nails."

That got Heather quiet!

I know my daughter hurts. I know she's anxious. I know she is good, all things considered, although she can be a bit of a Grumpysaurus. And I shouldn't compare her experience to mine. I had no one when I had my kids—no one cooking, no one doing laundry, no one staying up with me as I breastfed, no one serving me, no one to talk to. My mom was direly sick and couldn't be there when I had my boys, and she had died before my daughter was born. My husband didn't take one day off from work any of the four times, whereas Heather's husband has been hands-on and sympathetic.

I realize too I did something that the lactation lady with the long nails says is now "verboten." I would lie down while nursing, sometimes falling asleep, with the kid next to me—like my old cat did with her kittens. As a child, I watched litter after litter being nursed. My lactation expert was my cat, my childhood pet—Mittens. And furball that she was, she never smothered any of her offspring. Fortunately, I didn't either. I didn't roll over and crush a single one of my kids. All four made it. (Not that I'm advising nursing while lying down. Folks are more careful nowadays—that's good.)

Perhaps I was too harsh about the lactation expert's long nails. Because come to think of it, my lactation expert, Mittens, had claws too. Literally!

So grandmas learn. Nothing is set in stone. Knowledge changes old habits. The one constant is that a grandma wants what's best for her grandchild, and a mom wants what she deems best for her child—no matter the age of the mom or the age of the child. C'est la vie!

SOME DAYS ARE LIKE THAT

Jesse Neve

A T 8 A.M. THAT bright, sunny, mid-July morning, I gathered my crew: Sarah (8), Jon (7), Daniel (5), Ben (2), and Papa (my father, 56, who lived with us because of his early-onset Alzheimer's).

"Okay, today Jon and Daniel have their doctor's checkups."

I had barely gotten the news out of my mouth when Jon blasted, "Doesn't Daniel have to get shots when he's five?" Instantly Daniel burst into tears. Yes, I had forgotten that—though I think I would have presented it in a slightly different way than Jon's blunt declarative question. I tried to comfort Daniel, who was not only upset at the prospect of shots but mad at Jon for "reminding" me.

When our names were called, Papa decided to stay in the waiting room, which would prove to be a wise decision on his part. The five of us followed the unfamiliar and unfriendly nurse out of the waiting room. Apparently our regular, super-friendly nurse was on vacation.

Her first mission was to weigh and measure Jon and Daniel. Jon popped out of his shoes and hopped onto the scale. During this time, I was holding Ben, my purse, and the bag of books and snacks. Jon was excited to hear how much he weighed, and he bounced off the scale to make room for his brother.

Daniel was wearing tennis shoes, and he refused to take them off. I set Ben down (which sent him into a deafening fit of tears) and handed my bags to Sarah. Daniel was fervently pressing his feet into the floor, making it difficult to remove his shoes. When I finally succeeded, I lifted him up and he hung like a wet noodle as I set him on the scale. The whole time that he was crying and yelling, "No!" Ben was clinging to my waist and legs, crying to be picked up.

The nurse, clearly overflowing with empathy, rolled her eyes and chirped, "Five-year-olds don't act like this!"

Sarah peeled Ben off of my leg, and I picked Daniel up and stepped on the scale myself.

Aloud I read, "Okay, 182 minus . . ." then I set Daniel down on the floor and climbed on the scale alone. " . . . 128 equals . . ."

The nurse answered, "Fifty-four. Very good." A senior couple nearby had been watching our escapades, and the lady shook her head in amazement. "Now that's an experienced parent! Very impressive!"

As we made our way down the hall, I picked up Ben who was still crying. Daniel kept reaching up and trying to get me to carry him as well. Sarah was walking behind me, moaning and raving about how heavy the bags were and that she was going to die because she had to carry them. (Thankfully she did not.)

Jon climbed happily up into the chair and proceeded to tell the nurse how much he loves to get his blood pressure taken because it feels like his arm is going to blow up—but then it doesn't (again, thankfully). Next, it was Daniel's turn. After I lifted him into the chair, he held his arm tight against his body and wouldn't let the nurse touch him. Eventually I was able to pry his arm away enough to put it on. That started the cry and wiggle fest again, all the while yelling, "No!"

Daniel has had his blood pressure taken before, so it wasn't that he was afraid. I'm sure he was just thinking of the shots, and he was mad at the world because of it.

With brotherly love, Jon sincerely volunteered to take an extra blood pressure test for Daniel, but the nurse wasn't amused. She finally gave up and left us alone to wait for the doctor.

Dr. Burns is our favorite doctor. We've known him forever. He delivered our babies. He was literally the first person to ever see Daniel, so Daniel is always comfortable with this man. But not that day, with the shots looming over his head. I had to hold him down while the doctor checked him out. He refused to talk to Dr. Burns. He refused to open his mouth. Oh, and then, don't you know, we realized that Daniel had picked that day to go commando! So when the doctor checked him out, there was nothing under his shorts! I could just feel the "Mother of the Year" award slipping away . . .

Next, the boys needed to have their vision tested. We all trucked out into the hall where our ever-so-cheery nurse pointed at a vision chart, and Daniel (through his tears) was supposed to read the letters. I finally got him to whisper four of the letters, and that apparently sufficed.

We had saved the best for last. Daniel was in for four shots. He screamed and howled with the most amazing intensity. I have given birth and not been as loud as he was. Sarah, Jon, and Ben were cowering in the corner of the room with their hands covering their ears. Poor Daniel.

Daniel was still whimpering as we exited the exam room. He was walking unevenly, wearing only one shoe. We passed four nurses who were smiling and shaking their heads, saying, "Tough day, huh?" We picked up Papa in the waiting room, and the receptionist looked sympathetic (and relieved) as we left the building.

It was a tough day, but as we drove home, I was thankful that Jon had been really cooperative with the doctor and nurses. I was thankful that Sarah was able to play with Ben and talk to him when I was busy dealing with Daniel. I was thankful that our doctor is easygoing and doesn't get stressed out at such ordeals. We are all thankful that Daniel doesn't need any more shots until he's twelve and that the day was over.

At suppertime that night, when my husband, Dave, asked about our day's adventures, Daniel replied, "Dad, I got four shots today. It hurt and I cried."

Yep. Some days are like that.

LOCKED IN THE BEDROOM

Jessica Marie Baumgartner

I HAD JUST STARTED a new job. I was going through a divorce. I woke up late and needed to get my daughters to the babysitter before my shift, but there was no time.

"Girls, get up!" I ran into my daughters' room in our apartment and flung their closet door open. I pulled out a couple of dresses and threw them at my five- and three-year-old.

My youngest, Lexi, went into the bathroom, and my eldest followed me into my room. "Are you okay?" she asked.

"I will be once I get to work." I stumbled into my clothes and fought off fears of getting fired. Then I glanced up and saw my eldest leaning against the door—the door that always stuck and maintenance still hadn't come over to fix. "Anna, no!" I shouted as I heard the knob latch.

Her eyes went wide and she turned to try the handle. It stuck. She shook it but couldn't get the door open. "Oh no."

"What's wrong?" Lexi called from the other side of the door.

"The door." That's all I needed to say. For weeks, we had to avoid closing my door because the handle hated me. The girls knew this well.

"I'm sorry, Mommy." Anna's big brown eyes watered.

"It's okay baby." I bent down to hug her, but then Lexi whimpered like a puppy from the other side of the door.

My heart stopped. I was trapped in my bedroom with my baby girl stuck on the other side of the door. Panic struck me. I stood

132

and yanked at the handle. It stuck like gum to the bottom of a movie theater seat. No matter how much I twisted, shook, and pulled at the door handle, it was jammed. It may as well have been super-glued to the frame.

"I have to go to work." I started pacing. At least I have my phone with me, I thought. I grabbed my phone from the dresser and called the apartment supervisor, but no one answered. It was still too early.

"Why does my office have to open before everyone else? Eight is too early!" I stared at my phone clock. It was 7:15. Time was running out. There was no way I'd get the girls dropped off and get to work in time.

Lexi whimpered again. "Mommy, I'm hungry."

"I know, baby." I walked up to the door and brushed my fingers on the painted wood. The thought of being separated from my hungry little girl consumed me. I had to get to her. She was stuck out there. Alone.

I went to the closet and searched for something to help. Why don't I have a power drill or a crowbar in here? I asked myself.

My closet was full of clothes and decorations—nothing of use to escape our captivity. My heart beat harder and harder. I was so upset that I wished to wage war on the door separating me and my little girl. But I wouldn't let it stand between us anymore.

Then I spotted it. Below the sea of clothes, lying on the floor by my heels and boots, were my rollerblades. The stopper especially caught my eye. I grabbed it like a prisoner with a shovel. This was our only chance for survival. I was consumed by the moment.

I told Anna and Lexi to step back as I hacked at the door like a crazed ax murderer. Wood chips flew. I thumped again and again. Finally, the hole I carved out gave me enough room to reach around and attack the doorknob from the outside. It released its hold on us and the door opened.

I kissed my rollerblade and tossed it back in the closet. I picked Lexi up and hugged her tight. She giggled. "Mommy, you broke the door."

"I'd break anything for you." I laughed and ran my fingers through Lexi's hair.

Anna smiled. "Does that mean we can eat now?"

I knew there was no time, but I couldn't leave them just yet. I quickly fed the girls and tried to relax with them for a few minutes before driving to the babysitter.

It was harder than usual to leave them, but once alone in the car, I focused on getting to work and being honest about what happened. Maybe my new boss would understand. Sure, the company had a ninety-day grace period for new employees, and I had only been there for a couple of months, but maybe they'd make an exception... I was a single mother, after all, and they were a family business.

I missed the girls already, and I didn't know what we would do if I lost my job. I was terrified when I got to the building, but I walked in and got to my desk as quickly as possible. I glanced over and found that my boss's office was dark. He was late too!

He didn't make it in for another hour, and when he did arrive, he had brought everyone cookies. No one mentioned my late arrival, and better yet, I had a treat to calm my nerves. Then I got a call from the apartment asking for permission to have maintenance come in and look at my doorknob. I told them about the escape, and thankfully they gave me a new door at no charge. The work was finished by the time I got the girls and came home that night. We celebrated by ordering pizza.

What had started as my worst day in ages turned into a sweet success, complete with a door handle that didn't stick.

HAVE KIDS, THEY SAID. IT'LL BE FUN, THEY SAID.

"Mommy, I want a snack."

Night[mare] at the Opera

Jules Older

W HAT'S THE POINT OF being a parent if you don't use it
to inflict on your children all the cultural advantages you
hated when you were their age?

That's my adage, and that's why I use every family trip as an
opportunity to enrich my daughters' lives with things I know
they won't appreciate. We live in a town of under 200, so even a
trip to Podunk is a cultural adventure. "Oh look, kids—that's a
McDonalds!"

But it's on family vacations to the big city where parental cultural hegemony really kicks in. And, as in school or the army, there's
not a darned thing the little ones can do about it.

Or so I thought. But that was before I gave my daughters the
ultimate "believe me, you'll thank me later" cultural experience:
opera. In the fabled Sydney Opera House.

Oh, and not just any opera—"Kids, we got lucky. You're not
gonna believe this, but I managed to get us tickets to Madame
Butterfly!"

They continued to jump from one hotel-room bed to the other,
completely ignoring the tone of false heartiness I was trying so hard
to pass off as enthusiasm. My wife threw me a look that, despite
its brevity, managed to convey without so much as a misplaced
comma, "You lugnut, when are you ever going to learn? If I've told
you once, I've told you a thousand times—they're too young to be
dragged kicking and screaming into high culture."

136

But opera tickets are nonrefundable. And thus, we found our-selves sitting front and center when the curtain went up. At first, the majesty of it all sent the kids into a dazed, hushed silence. But even majesty wears off, especially when people are singing/screech-ing very loudly in extremely high voices. And even more especially when, from a strictly visual viewpoint, the romantic leads are so poorly matched.

Madame B. was no slender Asian reed. She was, in fact, a rather large Teutonic type who might be better cast as someone named Brunhilda and more comfortable wearing a horned helmet rather than a kimono. By contrast, the lovestruck Lieutenant—well, here's how Daughter A (I use the A to protect her identity, which is Amber Older) loudly reacted to him: "Why is that man so little?!"

In a voice that rivaled those onstage, Daughter W (a.k.a. Willow Older) asked, "Is he supposed to be her boyfriend?"

I shushed them both and nodded. In an even louder voice, Daughter A bellowed, "He's too old for her!"

Matching her decibel for decibel, her sister hollered, "And too small. Way too small. He's just a teeny-ween—"

My wife and I reached over to silence our progeny, but not before everyone sitting within a twenty-seat range did exact-ly the same. Between my daughters' critiques and a chorus of "Shhhhh's," you could no longer hear the singers.

But as so often happens in these situations, things rapidly got worse. Despite the threat of the "death by a thousand shhhh's" from the surrounding seats, plus a rapidly escalating series of parental warnings ("If you don't behave, we're leaving right this minute!" "YAY . . ." "Okay, if you say one more word, you're grounded for the rest of the century!" "How long's a century?"), my progenies' loud commentary continued unabated throughout the entire first act.

When we made for the exit at intermission, so did most of the people sitting around us.

I never did figure out whether they were leaving because of my daughters . . . or because they too were only there because someone made them go.

I WILL FIND YOU PEE SMELL

Heather G. Preece

MY ONE AND ONLY goal for the day was to find the source of the pee smell in the upstairs of my house. I would sit on my bed, nursing my newborn son, and catch a whiff of urine that would make my stomach turn.

Where is that coming from?! Is it a dirty diaper we forgot to throw away? Did one of the older boys wet their pants and leave them somewhere for me to find? Is this just a terrible case of bad aim? Potty-training problems still plagued my oldest, autistic son. And distracted by ADHD, my middle son had no time for such things as toilet breaks.

I was determined to solve the mystery by the end of the day and make my house fresh and clean again. In my best Liam Neeson voice, I said, "I will look for you, I will find you, pee smell, and I will kill you!" Maybe a little dramatic, but I couldn't stand one more day lying in bed smelling toilet smells!

I began my search under the bed. All I found there was a stash of empty Dr. Pepper cans—a conversation for another day with the four-year-old. Inhaling deeply, I ripped every sheet and pillowcase off every bed. Never had I ever wished for a bed-wetting incident before, but I was hoping it would be that simple. Nothing. I started scouring every toy, book, and game like some sort of drug-sniffing dog on all fours, trying to use my nose to detect the problem. I came up empty-handed once again.

The overpowering scent lingered during a break to feed the crying baby. I grabbed a bottle of Febreze from my nightstand. (When you live with all boys, trust me, you want Febreze on your nightstand.) Carefully spraying it away from my baby's face, I hope to inhale the fresh scent of lavender, but all I get is a whiff of a lavender-covered gas station bathroom. Time to resume my search!

I check the carpet, the shower curtains, the bath mats. Throw everything into the washing machine and scrub every nook and cranny around the toilet. The sound of the older boys fighting downstairs reaches me. Oh, lunchtime! Bad move. No one wants hangry children.

While I'm making peanut butter sandwiches, sudden noises come from upstairs. Leaving a half-made sandwich behind, I investigate where the noise is coming from. My oldest son is playing in his room, so that leaves my middle son. Who is he talking to? I crack the door open to see him with his pants and underwear on the floor, his back turned toward me, his front pointed at . . . not the toilet—the wall!

"What are you doing?!" I asked as I flung the door open. He turned around, midstream.

"Look, mom! I can spell my name!" he declared proudly as drops of liquid trickled down the wall . . . mystery solved.

A Dangerous Thing I Brought On An Airplane

Jennifer Companik

Dangerous Things One May Not Bring on an Airplane:

1. Liquids or gels in containers larger than three ounces outside of a clear, resealable, quart-sized zip-top container

2. Brass knuckles

3. Box cutters

4. Guns

5. Bombs

Dangerous Things One May Bring on an Airplane:

1. As many beverages from the duty-free shop as will fit in your carry-on luggage

2. Stiletto heels

3. Glass figurines

4. Tuna salad sandwiches

5. Young children

I would never bring a tuna salad sandwich or a bomb on an airplane, but I have brought a young child.

Spring break of 2008 saw me and my dairy-allergic four-year-old son (with as yet undiagnosed attention-deficit/hyperactivity disorder) conquering the sky. My husband couldn't take the week off, so it was just Son and me. That should have given me pause, but when it was a matter of spending all of March in the Midwest or visiting my mom in Florida for spring break, well . . . I probably would have agreed to tote my boy, your boy, all of Chicago's unhoused, and seven rabid raccoons in exchange for a week of sunny warmth.

Our trip commenced on St. Patrick's Day, which is an ideal day to travel—everyone goes to work, but people are, if anything, more jocular than usual. Thus we set out. Our flight was mid-day, our bellies full. After taking our seats, a woman stopped at our row with her seven-year-old son, Abdul, and what looked like ten other children to me but which might have only been three. She too lacked an adult travel companion. The woman told me the seat beside me was Abdul's assigned seat: Would I mind if he sat there? I'd never heard that one before. People on airplanes tend to plunk themselves into their assigned seats with zero concern for the preferences of their seatmates.

"Of course not," I said, and I meant it. For one thing, Son looked eager to talk to Abdul, and for another, I'm a schoolteacher and children do not, as a rule, frighten me.

Abdul's mom smoothed her son's hair, bade him behave, and opened an airsick bag on his lap.

Now that frightened me, but it was too late to object.

The plane flew. Son and Abdul played with Son's cars. Abdul read books about garbage trucks and cement mixers to Son. An hour into the flight, I hadn't broken a single sweat. Young bodies need to wiggle, so I took Son and Abdul on a "walk" through the "forest" to the bathroom and up and down the "path." People complimented me on my adorable "sons." When I explained Abdul was just our seatmate, fellow passengers' eyes widened with admiration. I spotted a red-headed, smiling baby wearing a St. Patrick's Day T-shirt, and she put her arms out. Her mom passed her to me, and I marched triumphantly down the aisle pumping Baby Irish up and down while she squeaked with delight.

When I got off the plane, I might've been a celebrity. People from the flight came up to me and told me how wonderful I was. I beamed from atop Maslow's hierarchy of needs.

Then I spent a week in a hotel room with Son, my mother visiting only briefly because she had to work. Ditto for my hometown friends. It could not have been that my kid was so insufferable, could it?

But how bad could a week at the beach be? You're absolutely right. Fort Lauderdale Beach, my hometown beach, cheered me enough that I withstood every tantrum and dirty look with equanimity.

Then came Easter Sunday. Time to take our tanned selves back to Illinois. Time to climb back on an airplane with Son. A 6 a.m. flight. The airport lay a half hour's drive from the hotel. I had to complete our packing, dress myself, rouse and dress Son, check out, drive to the airport, return the rental car, and arrive at the airport an hour before our flight. I didn't have to wake up until 3 a.m.

Have you ever had to wake up at 3 a.m. for a trip? You woke up at 2, didn't you? No? Just me?

I'm the kind of person who needs eight hours of unbroken sleep, yet there I was, yoked with Son and baggage and a time-sensitive to-do list on three hours of sleep. Did I mention it was a holiday? Easter. Know who works on Easter Sunday? NO ONE.

Everything I had to do took thirty, to fifty, to one hundred percent longer than it would have taken on any other day. But we made it to the airport at 5 a.m. as planned.

Breakfast. I could at least look forward to breakfast. And here's where I let you in on a secret about the Fort Lauderdale airport: The restaurants don't open until 6 a.m.

But I'm a mom. I pack snacks like cops pack heat. If you ever bump into me and are hungry, all you have to do is whine a little and I'll whip out a granola bar, or a piece of chocolate, or a lollipop, and a thermos full of Egyptian chamomile tea.

I had bagels. But thanks to the regulations surrounding liquids and gels, I lacked peanut butter. I'd sneaked in some hotel-buffet-sized packets of jelly, but Son didn't want jelly, he wanted peanut butter. One could, in 2008, find water and soda and aspirin in an airport vending machine but never peanut butter.

The hate stares from other passengers started before we got on the plane, after Son learned of the peanut butter situation. There was much wailing and gnashing of teeth—his and mine.

Then the flight was delayed an hour. My eyelids kept sliding shut against my will. I worked ineffectually to keep Son from poking at strangers while their hate grew stronger.

The restaurant in our terminal opened. I perused their offerings: everything but the fruit contained dairy. Son refused fruit. There was no peanut butter.

By the time we boarded the plane, I thought for sure Son would sleep until we got to O'Hare. He hadn't slept much more than I had. Maybe it would be okay.

Here's where I'll say . . . at least the plane didn't crash.

Turbulence kept us chained to our seats. Son sat at the window, I in the middle, and a man we didn't know sat in the aisle seat. Son showed no interest in sleeping—or sitting. He kept unbuckling himself and trying to run away. I had to wrestle him back into his seat and buckle his seatbelt no fewer than twelve times. Each performance of this operation brought me closer to, as parents say, completely losing it. By the third hour of the flight, Son had kicked, punched, scratched, spit on, and bitten me. I was literally bleeding. I held his ferocious body in his seat and wept.

It was then I realized that the man beside me was likely having the worst flight of his life because of my progeny. With my one free hand, I wrote him a sincere note of apology and signed it.

He wrote back, saying I needed "professional help" with my parenting, and that I was "much too pretty" to be crying. No signature.

His note consoled me in a way: My not prying his mouth open and pushing the anonymous note down his esophagus, into his stomach, and through his intestines proved that I had not, in fact, completely lost it. I focused on Son with renewed composure, and everyone survived the flight—though part of me wished I'd had a set of brass knuckles with which to educate the man in the aisle seat.

It May Sound Like Sleep... But it's Not.

Amilee Weaver Selfridge

M Y YOUNG SON ASKED me to have a sleepover with him. Being the cool mom I am, of course, I said yes. It's easy to say yes when your son is too young to know that a sleepover is anything different from sleeping in the same room together.

Oh, but I was wrong. Apparently, he learned about sleepovers from a TV show. I was not prepared to stay up talking all night like a couple of middle school girls!

Scratch that. I was not prepared to be kept awake by my son talking all night like he was a middle school girl.

I tried my hardest to stay awake, but it was just so hard! I would keep drifting off to sleep and then wake up to him right in front of my face, spouting off one life-altering question after another.

"Do sharks wear face masks?"

"If a shark ate a person with the virus [COVID], would they die of the virus?"

"You're a girl. Did you know that?"

"Do you have a mom and dad?"

"Mom, why do you make loud noises when you're asleep?"

"Why can't I understand what a dog is saying when it talks?"

"Do fish get thirsty?"

"Is Pac-Man real or cartoon?"

"Do cows have best friends?"

For hours, the questions kept coming.

Eventually, I really did fall asleep. It couldn't have been too long, but it was long enough to fall deeply asleep.

Suddenly, I shot up, being tapped awake to see two beady little eyes directly over me.

I held in a scream as my son whispered, "Mom, I'm tired now. Can I go to sleep?"

He then lay down and fell asleep instantly.

I stared at him shakily for a long time before my heart calmed down.

Sure glad *he* wasn't having any problem sleeping. (Insert sarcasm here . . .)

Word to the wise about sleepovers:

If you think it was hard being cool when you were young, just know that it's way harder when you're not so young anymore.

But most of all—it may sound like sleep . . . but it's not.

The Wake-Up Call

Jon Jones

"**J**on . . . Jon! Wake up! Get in here quick!"

I glared hazily at the ceiling and then stumbled out of bed. As I walked into the nursery, my wife, Kia, stared at our baby Nicole as she laughed and bounced in her crib.

Once my vision came into focus, I saw red and brown clumps resembling spaghetti and meat sauce in Nicole's crib, on her bedsheets, and on the wall. As I stepped closer, I noticed the substance in Nicole's hair, on her face, and even in her mouth. As my nostrils burned, the reality of the situation set in. "Is that . . . poop?"

"Yes! Agh! This is so gross! Oh my goodness!" Kia paced the floor as Nicole laughed and cooed with glee.

Our beautiful baby girl continued to paint and layer her crib like an artist with a canvas. Although her dedication to her craft was nothing short of inspirational, her final product was nothing short of disgusting.

My throat tightened. "What do we do?"

"Well, I'm gonna need you to either clean this room or bathe her. Which will it be?" Kia stood with her arms folded, awaiting my decision.

The options were very appealing, to say the least. Either take on the musty masterpiece on the crib and wall or disinfect a poop-encased infant. "Ugh. I'll just bathe her."

I reached into the crib and extracted Nicole, making sure not to allow even a drop of poop to touch me. Elbows fully extended, I rushed her down the hallway and into the bathroom.

After getting Nicole into warm bath water, I grabbed her hand towel and saturated it with more soap than it could hold. My eyes locked onto the chaotic nest of hair, and then I went to work. It took until my arms ached, but eventually, the matted mess broke apart and gave way to a sea of flowing black strands. The brown bath water drained down the tub like thick mud.

I gently wiped around her mouth and cheeks. Her face, once crusted and discolored, now revealed smooth, vibrant brown skin. Nicole smiled at me and cooed as if nothing had gone wrong.

After her bath, we returned to the nursery to get her dressed. To my relief, Kia finished scrubbing most of the room. The bright scent of lemon cleaning products had replaced the foul smell of the sewer system.

Afterward, Kia and I headed to the living room and crashed down on the couch. After cleaning Nicole and sanitizing the disaster zone, we enjoyed the sound of silence for the moment. However, as parents of an infant, we knew the peace wouldn't last. We knew we were destined for another beatdown at any given moment. Even though we experienced a full day's worth of chaos, the day had only just begun.

Mother's Guilt

Sarah Walker

I'M NOT A SUMMER-FARING lass. The heat is unbearable. At eight months pregnant, my body struggles to function. Still, I have a toddler who's full of energy, so it's not like I can rest when I need.

I've been feeling bad for my daughter—call it mother's guilt. She complains of boredom nonstop. My pregnancy combined with the overwhelming heat means we've been mostly cooped up indoors all summer. Yes, we visit the pool here and there, but we have to be cautious of the relentless sun on our pale, almost translucent skin. School starts in two more weeks, I remind myself. Breathe.

My daughter triggered my mother's guilt one morning when she asked me, "Are we going to stay at home forever? I want to go to the park."

I sighed and pinched the bridge of my nose. I wasn't sure if I could endure a walk to our nearest park. This late in my pregnancy, I was out of breath just from walking to the mailbox or climbing the stairs. Still, I didn't want to let my dear daughter down. So I took in another breath and, as a labor of love, I went through the trouble of walking her to the dang park.

I hoped I could avoid the worst of the heat by going while it was still morning. Of course, this was August in South Carolina, so it was still ridiculously hot. Regardless, I forced myself to make the trek. I worried about getting overheated and fainting. Thankfully, we did make it. Yet, on arrival, my daughter said, "I want to go home. It's too hot!"

By the time we made it back home, greeted by the welcoming embrace of the cool air conditioner, I was out of breath and felt like I was dying. I collapsed on our living room sofa. Then my daughter asked, "Mommy, why are you so tired?"

Mommy Meet-Up

Sarah Meade

After the birth of my first child,
I was eager to make new mom friends.
I loved staying home
with my sweet newborn son.
My life was full
of feedings,
diaper changes,
storybooks,
and singsong motherese.
Truly, this is what I'd dreamed of:
being a stay-at-home mom.
But I missed the camaraderie
and conversations that accompanied
my former job.
I was ready for some refreshing
adult conversation,
so I decided to venture out
with my little one.

My first mommy meet-up meant
nerves and excitement.
I picked a pretty top
to wear

and took some time
on my hair and makeup.
I chose a cute summer outfit
for the baby
and packed the diaper bag with care.
As I pulled up to the restaurant,
I took a deep breath.
I double-checked that I had
my purse, diaper bag, and phone.
Then I hopped out and
carefully extracted my baby boy
from his car seat.
He gurgled and cooed
as I snuggled him
against my chest in a baby carrier.

We went inside,
and I greeted the other moms.
There were about ten of us
and a dozen children,
some babies,
some preschoolers.
We ate lunch together
at a long table.
We chatted
about motherhood
and our daily lives.
I smiled at the kids
babbling and giggling.
I was feeling proud of myself
and happy I had ventured out that day.
All this time, I was wearing
my sweet baby in the baby carrier

and patting his back
through the thin fabric.
I felt comfortable and competent
as a new mom
out and about
with my little bundle of joy.
Then I heard some muffled sounds
and noticed the baby passing gas—
or filling up his diaper
more likely.
I proceeded to chat
for a few more minutes
with the other moms.
Then I smelled a familiar stench.

I hopped up to change
my son's diaper in the ladies' room.
When I got there,
I carefully unbuckled the baby carrier
to lay him on the changing table.
I gasped.
He was absolutely covered in poop.
All the way up his back
and around the front of his body.
Even down his little chubby baby thighs.
A real diaper explosion.
His sweet summer outfit?
Splattered and smeared in the most unsweet way.
Yuck!
I looked down at myself.
The cute top I'd chosen for this special outing?
Also covered in baby excrement.
Yikes!

I couldn't help it.
I burst out laughing
in the blessedly empty
public restroom.
I chuckled as my baby lay there—
all big eyes and innocent smile
amidst the soiled scene.
I pulled out my phone
to capture several pictures
of this messy moment.
I laughed
as I dabbed at my shirt
with wet paper towels.
The giggles continued
as I went to work changing
the baby and cleaning him up.
I used a lot of wipes.
A lot.
And I laughed
all the while I wiggled him
out of his soiled onesie.

Soon my baby was happy
and odor-free,
in a new diaper and fresh onesie.
I had packed a new outfit
for my little one,
but hadn't had the foresight—
or experience—
to pack an extra shirt for myself.
I improvised,
throwing a nursing cover

over my stinky shirt.
I cuddled my son in my arms,
and we fled the restroom
with the baby carrier
dangling around my waist.
I waved goodbye
to the other moms.
Some of the ladies looked
a bit puzzled
at my abrupt departure,
but I was too
embarrassed to explain.
I simply smiled
and made a beeline for my car.

The Fortune Teller And the Kid

Don Drewniak

W E TRAVEL BACK IN time to the 1950s, my favorite of the many decades I have had the good fortune of experiencing.

It was a hot and humid summer day following my being freed from second grade. I knew something unusual was about to happen when my mother, to use a popular fifties expression, was "dressed to the hilt."

"Come on, Donald. We're going to take a walk."

I panicked. "We're not going to the dentist, are we?"

"No, we're going someplace special."

That got my attention. "Where?"

"To a fortune teller."

"A what?"

"A fortune teller. Someone who can tell what's going to happen in the future."

"How far do we gotta walk?"

"Not far. Just to the other side of St. Elizabeth's Church."

"Okay."

"You'll need to put on your school clothes."

"Why?"

"Because this is someplace special."

I wasn't happy about having to change my clothes, but seeing a fortune teller made it okay. I thought I might be able to figure out how the fortune teller knew what was going to happen. Then

I could find out what would be on the tests at school and sell the answers to the dumb kids for a nickel.

As we walked along, I had visions of entering a palace, though I had never seen anything remotely resembling one anywhere near St. Elizabeth's, or anywhere else in my hometown of Fall River, Massachusetts.

My mother stopped walking ten houses past the church and said, "Here we are."

I stared in disbelief at a small, one-story house that looked like it was ready to be wrecked by my father. (Among the many jobs he had in the past was that of wrecking old buildings.)

Any hope that my mother had brought us to the wrong place was dashed by a cracked white sign with hand-painted stars and a crescent moon, topped with the name Madam Zarkova.

So much for getting rich.

"Mom."

"Yes, Donald?"

"I think the fortune teller stole her name."

"What do you mean?"

"She stole it from Doctor Zarkov."

"Who is Doctor Zarkov?"

"Are you kidding? Everybody knows Doctor Zarkov."

"Well, I don't."

"Betcha Dad does."

"I'm sure he does. Now who is he?" she asked again.

"The scientist in Flash Gordon."

"Well, I'm sure she didn't steal his name."

"Betcha she did."

She ended the conversation by knocking on the front door. Nothing happened. We waited. She knocked again. Nothing happened—again—so I turned the knob and pushed open the door.

"Donald!" scolded my mother.

"Well, shouldn't she know we're here?"

She had no answer for that and instead decided to walk into the small room, which was almost completely dark. No lights were on, and the shades were pulled all the way down, covering the room's only two windows. Trailing behind my mother, I resisted the temptation to make ghost sounds. To be honest, I was a little bit scared.

The room had four wooden chairs and a wooden table with a turned-off lamp on it. Nothing else.

While my mother was debating whether we should sit down, there was a creaking sound accompanied by the slow opening of a door opposite the entrance to the house.

In walked Madam Zarkova. She wasn't much taller than my Grandma Sophie who was slightly under five feet, but she was considerably heavier. Covering her entire body was a black robe covered with stars and a bunch of crescent moons. She had some kind of black cloth wrapped around her head.

I figured her hair was wet.

"Welcome. And who do we have here?" she asked while looking at me.

"This is my son, Donald."

"Hello, Donald."

"Hi."

"And your name is?" she asked my mother.

"Catherine."

I wondered why she didn't already know our names.

They briefly engaged in small talk before we were ushered into the fortune-telling room. It was almost as dark as the first room. The only window was covered with a black velvet curtain that blocked out all but a sliver of light from entering the room. A dim lamp in the corner of the room and a few candles were the only other sources of light.

My mother sat on a chair in front of a round table covered with a black tablecloth that extended down to the floor.

Madam Zarkova sat opposite my mother. I was relegated to a far corner of the room. I'm sure Madam Zarkova would have preferred me not to be in the room at all.

My mother paid up front. It was obvious she didn't want me to know how much she was paying as she kept her back to me so I couldn't see the exchange of money.

I wish I could definitively say whether there was a crystal ball on the table, but I can't remember.

Madam Zarkova spoke in a whisper, as did my mother. No matter how hard I tried to listen, I could only pick up an occasional word or two. The only words I remember are "handsome stranger" and "Cadillac." At the time, I don't believe I knew what handsome meant. My parents never owned a Cadillac, and to the best of my knowledge, they never associated with anyone who drove one.

As we were leaving what had been a very disappointing visit (for me at least), Madam Zarkova made the mistake of telling me that if I wanted to ask one question, she would be glad to answer it.

Before thinking about it, I blurted out, "If you can tell what's going to happen, how come you live in a junky house?"

"Donald!" admonished my mother.

Madam Zarkova glared at me. It was a good thing she wasn't a witch, or I might have been turned into a frog or a rock.

On the way home, I asked my mother how much she paid Madam Zarkova.

"Twenty-five cents."

I knew that was going to be told to Father Tell-Me-All-Your-Sins the next time she went to confession.

We walked a few more steps before she said, "Donald, I really should tell your father about your disrespect."

The tone of her voice implied that she wouldn't tell him what I said to Madam Zarkova—if I wouldn't squeal about her going to see a fortune teller.

Without another word being spoken, the bargain was made and honored.

SOMETHING RIPPED RIGHT NEXT TO MY HEAD

Jesse Neve

"MOM! MOM!" I HEARD his little voice as I was torn from a peaceful slumber. I struggled to open my eyes as I rolled over and leaned toward my young son. "Mom! Something ripped right next to my head!"

My foggy brain could not compute what he was telling me.

"What, Jon?" I blinked repeatedly and shook my head to try to gain clarity.

"I don't know. But there was a loud rip right next to my head!"

I swung my feet around the side of the bed. I was used to this sort of night. Our kids were one, three, five, and seven, so there was never a night where we didn't have some kind of action. But something ripping? What could that be?

My mind wrestled with the possibilities as I followed little Jon back into the room that he shared with his three-year-old brother, Daniel. What could be going on?

It all became clear when I flipped on the light. Daniel had thrown up over the side of the top bunk, past Jon's head below, where it splatted onto the floor. Jon had perceived the unusual sound to be a rip when indeed it was more of a splat.

Needless to say, it was a long night.

IT SEEMED LIKE A GOOD IDEA AT THE TIME

"Now that I finally have it all, I'd like to give some of it away."

WHY I'M NOT ALLOWED IN THE PET STORE ANYMORE

Christina Gochnauer

S o . . . background information. I am an animal person. I have never met an animal I didn't want to be friends with. I like animals more than most people.

My husband, on the other hand, is not so much an animal person. I didn't realize how drastically we differed in our opinions of an appropriate number of animals living in a home until we adopted five animal-loving children who want to keep every stray anything they find. We have four dogs—which he feels is at least three too many—a turtle, two goldfish, and at any given time, tadpoles hatching in a tank somewhere.

With that context, you might understand why my sweet husband—who, as much as he dislikes having so many animals, adores his family—would feel nervous when I announced we were going to a pet store.

To be fair, I had already given my four-year-old daughter a lecture on how we would absolutely not be bringing home one more animal before walking into the pet shop to look at the pretty fish and pet the bunnies. I had promised I would not be buying anything at the store. And to be perfectly fair, we didn't. But . . .

My little one and I were walking hand in hand toward the bunnies when a woman asked if we'd like to pet her puppy. Of course we would! A tiny ball of fluffy miniature Australian shepherd whined and licked our hands as we petted his soft fur. We were both enchanted.

"Would you like to hold him?" the woman asked my tiny four-year-old, who immediately made grabby hands toward the woman and was rewarded with an armful of wiggly happy pup. She plopped down on the floor and let the pup snuffle her hair and lick her face. So. Cute. The woman gushed about how sweet they looked together and I agreed wholeheartedly. "Would you like to keep him?" she asked us.

I thought she was joking. She had to be. Who just gives away an Australian shepherd puppy in a pet store that doesn't even sell puppies? This stranger is who.

I hemmed and hawed for a minute while my child wrapped her arms tightly around her newest friend. I was assaulted by two pairs of adorable puppy eyes, only one of which belonged to an actual puppy.

The woman said she'd buy us a crate, leash, collar, bowls, and food if we'd take him. She had bought him a week before in a nearby city, and she realized she didn't have time for him but didn't want to take him to the shelter.

I am only human, y'all. While knowing I was agreeing to something my husband would absolutely not approve of, I found myself nodding in agreement. Someone with a significantly stronger resolve would have needed to be there to pry the puppy from my daughter's arms at that point. We loaded ourselves into the van, my little girl happily chatting with her new bestie.

I called my husband to prepare him emotionally. "Um . . . so I need you to promise not to be angry." As my husband is not prone to anger as a rule, he was naturally concerned. "It's not bad. But you might be angry. Just, uh . . . I'm almost to your work. Come outside."

He came outside, a concerned look etched on his face. I opened the van door where he was greeted with the sight of a giggling four-year-old holding a tiny Australian shepherd puppy on her lap who was gleefully licking her nose. Naturally, he had some questions.

To be honest, I still had questions. Regardless, he grudgingly agreed it would have been hard to say no.

We're now five years past that day, and the kiddo and pup are still the very best of friends. My husband does not love the dog. But he adores our kids, so he tolerates him. And even though I'm an adult and am allowed to do whatever I want, he's kindly asked me not to go to the pet store without adult supervision.

Kitty's Very Bad Day in the Loo

Rose Florian

M Y MOM, KITTY, AS she was known, was constantly clean-ing our house. She dusted, vacuumed, and scrubbed every inch of every room.

Kitty was especially particular about keeping a clean kitchen and bathroom.

One summer afternoon in the mid-1970s, I came home to find Mom sitting in her favorite living room chair, her feet elevated on an ottoman, reading the local newspaper, the Fall River Herald News. This was unusual since she never relaxed in the afternoon; her time to relax was always in the evening after supper.

"Hi, Mom, what's up? Finally taking a break?"

"No, hon, I have to keep my swollen ankles and feet up."

I looked at her ankles and noticed bruising. I began to panic.

"Mom, what happened?"

"I had a bit of an accident today."

"What kind of accident? Did you fall?"

Mom then explained. She had been "deep" cleaning the bath-room. This meant that everything in the bathroom was scrubbed thoroughly. Our bathroom was of average size for our house, a two-bedroom cottage that was built by my dad, Jan.

There was a window in one of the walls, and the space between that wall and the toilet was very narrow, approximately six to eight inches wide. Mom was only five foot two (157 cm), so in order for her to clean the window, she had to stand on a step stool that she placed in front of the toilet. She then would stretch her body over the toilet and reach up high to clean the window.

Mom couldn't find the step stool that day. She told me she blamed my dad for misplacing it. I found this odd since I had no recollection of ever seeing him use the step stool. He was tall enough to reach up to the top of the windows.

Mom decided she would try standing on the toilet seat cover to reach the window. With glass cleaner and wiping cloths in her hands, she stood with both feet on the toilet seat cover and began stretching up to the window.

Before she could comprehend what was happening, her body dropped and both feet and ankles were jammed inside the toilet. Mom started screaming for help, hoping beyond hope that someone would hear her. Dad couldn't have heard her because he was deaf. She couldn't move her lower body at all, and her upper body was swaying this way and that way. Then she heard a loud crash. She was able to turn her head slightly, just in time to see that the toilet seat cover had flown into the living room and crashed into the wall.

Dad subsequently explained to me the reason for the delayed flight of the toilet seat cover, but the explanation has long since departed from my memory.

Fortunately, Dad was outside talking with our next-door neighbor Rick, who heard Mom screaming. He grabbed Dad's arm and pulled him into the house. Rick's wife, Eileen, heard the commotion from inside her house, so she ran over as well. According to Mom, this was Dad's reaction:

"Kitty! What the heck are you doing?"

"I'm stuck! Help me! Get me out of here, people! I'm stuck in the toilet!"

"Boy, oh boy . . . you sure did it this time, Kitty."

"Never mind, you! Just get me out of this toilet!"

It took the two men quite a while to free Mom from the toilet. Dad had to get a hammer to break the toilet top cover while Rick and Eileen held on to Mom to prevent her from falling over.

They finally lifted Mom up and out. By this time, her ankles and feet had become numb, so the three of them held her up and put her in her favorite chair.

Eileen got a bucket, filled it with cold water and ice, then put Mom's feet in it. She placed a cool towel over Mom's legs and waited until the numbness subsided.

Eileen told me later that day that Dad and Rick immediately left once Mom was in her chair. She then brought Mom a glass of water and aspirin and then made her a cup of tea. She looked out the window, not the least bit surprised to see Dad and Rick laughing their heads off.

Her first thought was to run outside and give the men a hard time for laughing, letting them know that Mom could have been seriously hurt. But on second thought, she started laughing as well. She though to herself, "Oh no! I can't let Kitty know we're all laughing at her."

Within a week, Mom was able to walk without a problem.

One evening several weeks later, Dad, Mom, Rick, Eileen, and I sat outside. The joking and laughing went on for quite a while. Fortunately, Mom was always good-natured and loved a good laugh.

"Kitty, you cost me a lot of money and work because of that dumb thing you did," admonished my father.

"Well, you took my step stool—it's all your fault."

On and on it went, all in good humor.

Mom threatened all of us, stating, "Under no circumstances are any of you to tell anyone about my accident. If I find out you did, you'll be very sorry."

I can't speak for the others, but I kept that promise.

Until now.

The Unforgettable Airport Adventure

Laura Niebauer Palmer

RUNNING THROUGH A BUSY airport with chunks of vomit rolling down my back was not the way I saw my spring break trip kicking off. But that's where I found myself, holding a vomiting three-year-old and ping-ponging amongst horrified passengers, all grateful they were witnessing the sight before them rather than partaking in it.Relief rushed over me as I reached my destination, the family restroom, and the handle easily turned in my hand.

What I was not expecting was the shriek from the woman in the vulnerable pants-around-the-ankles position. As we locked eyes, her mouth formed an O as I quickly apologized.

Slamming the door shut, I rushed past the line of weary travelers waiting for the main restroom.

As the torrent ceased, I took inventory of us in the mirror. Looking back was a frazzled mom with streaks of vomit down the front and back of her sweatshirt and an exhausted kiddo equally covered in throw-up.

It was hard to believe that just hours earlier, the child in my arms had been playing outside, full of energy, displaying no signs of what was to come. The only clue that something was amiss was when we arrived at the airport and he didn't finish his pizza—and turned down the offer of ice cream.

He always finished his pizza.

And he always said yes to ice cream.

He had never thrown up in the three years of his existence, so we had little to go on.

After I discarded my sweatshirt in the bathroom trash and changed my son's clothes, we returned to the gate where my husband was on all fours attempting to clean up red-colored mush.

The morning strawberry binge had come back to haunt us.

"How are you feeling, buddy?" my husband asked.

"Better," came the reply.

"Alrighty, let's board," said my husband.

"You aren't seriously thinking of still going?" I asked.

"It's just nerves; he'll be fine," he insisted.

With seconds to decide, I fought against every rational thought pinging around in my mind and acquiesced.

As soon as we took our seats, a look came over my son.

My hand fumbled for the barf bag in the seat pocket, but I was too late.

With one hand covered in vomit, I used the other to push the call button, summoning an unsuspecting flight attendant.

"We need to get off this plane," I said, nodding toward my son as an explanation.

To his credit, the flight attendant was a complete pro. As he ushered us off the plane, I kept apologizing, knowing that we would go down in the annals of flight attendant lore as "those people."

When we returned to the gate, I planned to clean up our son while my husband retrieved the car. Just before he was swallowed up by the multitude of travelers, it hit me.

The car seat. It had been checked.

"Wait, we need the car seat!" I yelled.

I explained the situation to the gate agent, who clearly did not want any part of my problems.

"Ma'am, there's nothing we can do. The bags will go through to your final destination," came her rehearsed response.

On cue, another string of red vomit exploded from my son.

Seeing the desperation in my eyes peeking out from the strings of vomit-clumped hair, she softened.

"Let me see what I can do," she responded as she radioed to the plane.

"What do your bags look like?" she asked.

Black.

They were all black, including the car seat cover.

Of course they were.

With a sigh, she got back on the radio.

Through the static, I heard the response that they could only pull the car seat; the rest would go through to our final destination. I wanted to cry in relief, but I knew that once I started crying, I wouldn't be able to stop.

We headed to the baggage claim with a bathroom pit stop to change my son's clothes—again.

Handing my son to my husband, I approached the counter and saw the look in the desk clerk's eyes—fear mixed with wonder at the sight in front of her. I could only imagine what we looked like.

Trying to keep a respectable distance, I began to explain the situation. Once again, as if perfectly timed, my son threw up, except my husband's back was the target this time. At this point, I wasn't even fazed. I grabbed the handful of paper towels I had stuffed in my backpack at the last bathroom stop while my husband headed to the restroom with our son.

Except we had no more changes of clothing.

Wishing him Godspeed, I turned my attention back to the airline worker. Her eyes widened as her walkie-talkie came to life.

As she was being debriefed on our situation, I spotted my husband walking toward me, both him and our son shirtless. Apparently, you can only do so much cleaning while keeping one hand under the censor, which releases a tiny squirt of soap and an on-and-off spray of water.

Taking in the spectacle before her, she told us they had pulled the car seat and our luggage and were on their way.

So there we were, either shirtless or covered in vomit. While I consider myself quite adept at chitchat, I had nothing to say. The scene spoke for itself.

Finally, the car seat and two of our three pieces of luggage arrived. As I profusely thanked the woman, my son threw up a fifth time as a parting gift.

Thankfully the worker took pity on me and waved me forward, insisting she would take care of it.

As I sat in the back seat with my son, the adrenaline that had propelled me for the past hour began to wear off, and I started to laugh uncontrollably.

"Did all of that just really happen?" I asked as I again noticed the drying clumps of vomit in my hair, confirming it indeed had.

Later that night, I checked my email while my son rested.

There was an email from the airline informing me that my reservation was canceled and their no-show policy went into effect, meaning we lost the money we spent on the flights.

As I emailed the customer service department detailing the day we had, I wondered how this story ranked amongst the countless tales they'd heard from travelers who had missed their flights.

Did it even crack the top ten?

The next day, we received a voucher for a future flight.

Either the representative on the other end of the email was a parent who took pity on me, or else they were a child-free one who probably remained so after reading my plight.

As for our son, by the next day, he was completely fine.

But we will never be.

WATCH YOUR WORDS CAREFULLY

Amilee Weaver Selfridge

I DIDN'T UNDERSTAND. THERE'S no way he could have misunderstood me.

I stared at my son, wondering how we possibly got to this moment.

My eyes glanced from my son, chewing dramatically, to the table where all his food sat on the table. Literally *on* the table. All of it. My eyes looked back up to my son as he stuck the last little piece of his paper plate into his mouth.

Yep, you heard me right. His paper plate.

He ate it. In fact, he swallowed the very last bit of it as I tried to catch up to the moment and make sense of what was happening.

Exasperated, my son spoke up, "Mom. You told me I could have my donut after I finished my whole plate. I finished it. Where's my donut?"

Trapped by logic, and faced with his valid argument of "I did exactly what you told me to, Mom," I handed my son his donut, realizing that as a parent, I would need to watch my words much more carefully.

Words are a dangerous thing when children are around.

A Wonderful Day

Kay Lesley Reeves

I WOKE MY HUSBAND early but with a fair amount of urgency that morning. The labor pains had started, and I knew from experience that my births were mercifully short.

The first time, he had suffered alongside me and tells me his hands still carry the scars to prove it. This time, he had the easier role. While I screamed and cursed in the bedroom, he had only to entertain our sixteen-month-old daughter, preferably somewhere well out of her earshot. At that age, toddlers are remarkable for their ability to learn undesirable words and repeat them loudly at exactly the wrong moment.

I managed to hold out while he gave her breakfast, but by the time she had eaten and redecorated the kitchen walls with baby food, I knew it was time to call the midwife.

Watching my husband trying to insert a wriggling, giggling toddler into an all-in-one waterproof coverall kept my mind off the pain for a good ten minutes. As the midwife arrived, I waved the two of them off, even though it was raining steadily. This left me free to settle down to the serious business of pushing our second daughter out into the world.

A tactful time later, after the noisy and messy bits were safely over, Baby and I were getting to know each other when I heard the front door open cautiously.

Having established that it was safe, two figures entered the bedroom, positively sparkling with happiness. As they gave a cursory glance at the beautiful baby I had so cleverly produced, I had time to have a good look at them.

Both were damp and distinctly muddy. My daughter appeared to have been dipped in chocolate and topped with a lovely sticky layer of cotton candy. They had found the local funfair and clearly had the time of their lives.

Between them, they babbled happily about swing boats, round-abouts, and the bouncy castle. They had ridden on the round-about and tested the dodgem bumper cars. They didn't need to tell me what they had eaten, as the evidence was all over their faces.

My husband confessed that he had been the recipient of several horrified looks as he carried our exhausted child back home. Luck-ily he understood how much more important her joy was than a bit of dirt.

Later that day, after the two had shared a warm bath and were clean and dry, the four of us snuggled up together. We were wrapped in a glow of love and contentment.

Over many years, our gorgeous daughters have brought us so much happiness, but I will always remember that very special day, never failing to smile at the memory of my beautiful new daughter and her delightfully dirty big sister.

Rain Date

Michele Herman

F OR OUR SON'S THIRTEENTH birthday, all he asked for was an overnight camping trip with a few friends. We reserved a site at Harriman State Park, a short ride up the Palisades Parkway. We invited a dad with a car, rented a second car, and borrowed a few tents.

As we turned onto the West Side Highway that Saturday morning, the firewood in the trunk tenderly cushioned with sleeping bags and marshmallows, we were feeling fine. When you live in Manhattan and don't have a car, you rely more than you like to—more than is entirely healthy—on your local car-rental place. Sometimes we arrive at the time of our reservation and they say, "Sorry, no cars." Sometimes we argue about which insurance coverage we need. The last time we got a car just fine but also got a $100 parking ticket during the minute it took to walk the luggage from the office to the trunk, fueling our suspicion that the car-rental place is a dummy operation set up by the local precinct across the street so they can make their monthly ticket quota without leaving the block. But on this auspicious day, we got out with no ticket and with a major upgrade, because even though we'd specified an economy, the only car left on the lot was a big fat convertible.

Actually, we weren't doing so fine. We had already postponed the trip once because of rain. Now it was one of those spring days of indeterminate temperature but alarming clamminess that sits like oilcloth on your skin. The Hudson River was gunmetal gray.

The really nice dad with the car was just behind us with half the guests, looking quite cheery for a guy who, as soon as he dropped off the kids, had to go back to the city for his daughter's dance recital and then drive back up in the morning to pick them up.

Meanwhile, back in our car, I was in the passenger's seat nursing a broken elbow, the result of a bike accident a few weeks before. Our younger son in the back seat, in an act of extreme recycling, was vomiting into the very bags that had held the week's groceries. I was not far behind, what with the trace anesthetics still coursing through me from the surgery to wire my elbow back together. And one more thing: New Yorkers may remember that retaining wall on upper Riverside Drive that collapsed so dramatically on the local news. This was right after that. The highway was open, but with the closed lane and the rubbernecking, we were making, oh, a mile an hour.

Luckily, we had an escape hatch—or rather a button with a little icon showing a raised convertible top. Unfortunately, there was no owner's manual in the glove compartment, and none of us had ever been in a convertible before. Were there things one had to know and do before pushing that button? The kids were looking to us for grown-up wisdom. We decreed: If we ever make it onto the Palisades Parkway (a possibility that seemed remote), we'll go for it.

Eventually, we crossed the bridge to Jersey, still moving slowly. Keeping our promise, I pushed the button. A motor whirred, and the roof of the car began its ascent. Clammy air rushed in. Vomity air rushed out. We cheered. But then the roof, at its apex, stopped—as if it thought we were in an amphibious vehicle and it was supposed to double as the mainsail. I stood up and tried to budge it, but it was too high and too unyielding.

There was no shoulder on the road, and at this point, the traffic began to flow quickly. I pushed the button really hard. I pushed it in a more staccato style a bunch of times in a row. I paused, giving the button a chance to regain its temper or let the gasoline drain away or whatever buttons need to do when they're not working. I pushed it afresh. Nothing changed, in that way that makes you generalize and believe that nothing ever will. We feared we'd broken some basic life rule that everybody knows but us, like "Don't wash your electrical outlets with soap and water."

Finally, the Yonkers scenic overlook came along. We motioned madly to the other car to turn off. As we pulled into the parking lot, the roof finally started folding and the window began a slow descent into its hidden chamber. (Major sighs of relief all around.)

You know how bad news comes in threes? Let's review. So far, we had a broken elbow and a broken retaining wall. Next came a broken window. (Major screams of fear all around.)

I was under the mistaken, or maybe outdated, impression that convertibles have plastic rear windows. This window was glass, and not safety glass. When it broke, it didn't break into those special rounded safety shards you see glittering on the street in bad neighborhoods like aquamarine birthstones. This window broke into regular malevolent shards. They ricocheted off the rear of the car and poured into the back seat.

After we plucked up the proverbial million little pieces and got back on the road, the camping trip got better—or so I'm told, because my younger son and I spent most of it in a fetal position moaning. This left plenty of s'more fixings for the others. We had time to bungee a tarp over the car and get cozy in our tents before the real rain started. The next morning, the air was clean and fragrant, and we picnicked at the pristine summit of Bear Mountain. And when we got back, windswept, to the city, our luck improved: No one vomited, and it turned out we had taken the kind of insurance that covered windows.

GET OUT OF HERE!

Jesse Neve

I T WAS THE MIDDLE of the night when two-year-old Jonathan silently climbed into our bed with us. My husband David was fast asleep, but I had heard Jon jump down from his big-boy bed and come into our bedroom. I opened the covers and let him snuggle up against me. He fell asleep almost immediately. This was our latest phase. It was cozy and nice to have him join us occasionally.

In the morning, my husband was the first one to awaken. I heard him and lay quietly, not wanting to disturb our little Jon stretched out beside me. David pulled back the corner of the curtain to check on the weather. Apparently, the first thing he saw was a stray dog mulling around our backyard. Quickly he hopped out of bed and yelled out the window. "Get! Get out of here! Get out! Get! Get!"

Jon snapped awake and took off running toward our bedroom door. It was like in the cartoons where the character's feet are spinning in mid-air before he tears away at top speed. Jon was out the door and back in his bedroom before Dave even realized he had been in our room.

By the time we were all caught up, Jon was long gone. We found poor Jon in his bed with wide eyes. We both joined him and poured our hugs and love on him. Looking out of Jon's window, we saw the stray dog trotting merrily down the street—the day little Jon thought he was being shooed out of our bed.

CHEESECAKE

Karl Stevenson

E VERY SUNDAY, MY COUSINS would begin recapping the latest cartoon episodes they saw on Cartoon Network. I would then get a look as they waited for me to jump in. I would do my best to avoid eye contact and hope the conversation would just move on. But with every face turned in my direction, I eventually had to say, "My mom doesn't let me watch Cartoon Network. She says it's too crazy and violent."

If I had a dime for every family member or classmate I had to tell that I didn't get their *Johnny Bravo* reference, I could have bought a multimillion-dollar home by age eighteen. Without having the same taste in shows, sometimes certain kids wouldn't let me play with them because I wouldn't fit in. My mother insisted I would thank her one day. She even stated that if she heard from a family member that I watched a show she didn't agree with, then my TV-watching privilege would be taken away for a week.

I'm sure you're curious what I *was* able to view. My Rolodex of shows that weren't banned primarily came from PBS and Disney. However, similar to other parents, my mother got tired of seeing the same episode on repeat and hearing the high-pitch theme songs that resonated throughout the house. She stated that I could watch TV with her and would point to the loveseat, encouraging me to join her.

One thing my mother didn't consider is that children tend to repeat whatever their ears have picked up. I walked into school the following day and approached the same kids who said I couldn't play with them.

"Hey Chris, go to sleep and pray for brains," I snickered.

"It's so nice not see you, Samantha—you're one chromosome away from being a potato," I whispered.

"Well, well, well. Look what the cat cleaned up, showered, exfoliated, powdered, lipsticked, and dragged in," I chuckled while motioning to Nicole.

My mom did not enjoy receiving a call from my teacher explaining that *Golden Girls* and *Will and Grace* may not be suitable for a nine-year-old.

PARENTING IS LIKE CHESS. I DON'T KNOW HOW TO PLAY CHESS.

"I thought you said chess was fun, Daddy. Why are you crying?"

Parenting Pros and Cons

L. Jade

I THINK EVERY PARENT hits that one critical moment where they remember life before kids. The nostalgia hits harder than a freight train and thoughts start pouring in, making you question why you thought having kids was a good idea in the first place.

For example, remember being able to get up and go whenever you wanted to wherever you wanted? Trip to the beach? Sure! Going to the store for some random thing? No problem! Want to get out of town for a weekend just because? Sounds great! Now you're lucky if you remember to pack enough diapers (let's not even mention wipes), and God have mercy on your soul if you forget the snacks. Doesn't matter if the tiny crumb-snatcher has just had lunch, he will get hungry while you're out.

Or perhaps it was having a set sleep schedule and bedtime routine. Taking a nice long shower, relaxing on the couch awhile, then moseying off to bed when you feel like it, knowing you don't have to get up until your alarm goes off the next morning. Or you can just sleep on the couch—no need to lose your comfort! Except if you even dared try that now, your tiny bundle of joy will wake you up. Again . . . and again . . . and again . . . until you're glad when the sun starts peeking out. The nightmare is finally over (even if you didn't really sleep to begin with).

Oh, but that nightmare isn't as horrible as the others. Accidentally leaving your kid in the middle of nowhere in his stroller as he screams to the heavens. Seeing your drowned child being pulled out of the lake when you couldn't find him fast enough after he fell in. Having your kidnapped child wondering where Mommy and Daddy are and why they abandoned him. Makes you wish for those "I forgot to study / do my homework" dreams instead.

So as you sit there and think of all this, other gems start twinkling in your mind: what a warm meal was like, when was the last time primary colors hadn't vomited all over the living room, when you didn't have to go to a doctor's office monthly (or weekly when your tot is pooping his guts out and having diaper rash to boot), not feeling extreme guilt for buying something for yourself instead of the kid. (I mean really, you don't have time to play those video games anyway . . .)

Why do we do this to ourselves again?

All right, those giggles are pretty cute, especially if there's a burp installed somewhere in the middle. Or if you're pretending you can't find your "hiding" love, and he thinks it's the absolute funniest thing, and everyone in the tristate area could easily pinpoint his location via squeals.

Watching him learn about himself and the world is pretty great too. I was never quite sure doors are entertaining, but wow, has my mind been blown! And the straps for the high chair, car seat, and swing? Oh, don't even get me started! Stairs are pretty great too. There's also been learning the rule of no hats or glasses for anyone, with rule-breaking reprimands such as the offending object being violently displaced from your person.

Also, let's not forget a good meal ends with throwing what you have left on the floor. I mean sure, smashing plates is fun, but food throwing is where it's at.

The joy I get when he learns something new is pretty amazing too. Crawling, mumbling, singing (all right, so maybe this is more like yelling, but still, he's got the spirit), pull-to-standing, rolling over, and walking (or close to it) are all milestones that cement themselves in your heart. Serotonin and dopamine really are a heck of a hormone cocktail.

And that smile. The cheeky one he gives when he's up to something, the sunshine-filled grin he throws your way when you walk through the door as he hauls his tiny butt as fast as he can over to you, the "I'm going to cause so much trouble" sly look . . .

So that being said, would I give it all up to regain my childless life?

Of course not. All of the no. Maybe that makes me crazy, but I think it's even crazier to ask such a question.

But I suppose that's what being a parent is all about.

Giving up your sanity to make room for love for your little.

Parenting is weird.

Never Brake A Promise

Peter Lewis Ebbitt

CHAPTER ONE

I was tinkering with my old Ford, replacing the air filter and replenishing essential fluids, when this whole affair began. I'm not certain, but I'm pretty sure I was humming. It was then my wife came out of the house.

"Are you ready to go?" she asked with a smile.

Having been married eighteen years, I knew better than to ask. I rolled with the query like a seasoned professional.

"Almost," I answered nonchalantly.

"You have no idea what I'm talking about, do you?" she asked.

It was obvious I had missed something . . . but what? We were married on my birthday, so I generally didn't screw that up. It must have been something I promised, but for the life of me, I couldn't remember what it was. I decided to improvise. Take it on the fly using real-time thinking, so to speak. It didn't work.

I started with "Of course I know what you're talking about, Honey . . ."

She cut me off. "Quit fooling around. You're taking your daughter for a driving lesson today. Remember?"

I suddenly felt lightheaded, lost my grip on the heavy air filter cover I was holding, and dropped it squarely on my foot. And even though it really, really hurt, I didn't scream. That can happen when you go into shock.

I desperately stammered, "No, no, dear. We both agreed she would learn to drive when she was sixteen and a half," I finished calmly.

"She was seventeen two months ago," replied my wife. "Put your car back together and give your daughter a driving lesson."

With hopes of rearranging my wife's thinking, I followed her in the house. If this didn't work, I could always faint and break my ankle.

"Honey," I said sweetly, "Be reasonable. She's just a little girl. Remember the time we ran into that maniac? He jumped out of his car and threatened me with a gun! You wouldn't want that to happen to our baby girl, would you?"

"As I recall," she said, "*you* were the one who jumped out of the car screaming at that man. And he didn't have a gun—it was a newspaper."

"It was *The Sunday Times*," I said, defending myself. "He could have been carrying a shotgun in a paper that size. And I clearly remember him saying he was gonna shoot my butt off," I finished confidently.

"No, dear, he called you a butthead because you cut him off. He was waiting for that parking spot you rushed into."

"That parking spot was fair game," I said resentfully. "If I had my pistol, he wouldn't have pulled a stunt like that."

"If you had had that stupid toy of yours, he would have beat the snot out of you. He was twice your size. And it's not a pistol, it's a BB gun," she said sarcastically. "That's why I don't want you carrying that thing around in the car. You'll wind up pointing it at the wrong person and get yourself shot with a real gun."

"It is not a BB gun, it's a pellet *pistol*. And it was good enough to take care of the Gronemans' dog, wasn't it?"

"How about we get back to the subject at hand?" she said stubbornly. "Teaching your daughter to drive?"

"Nobody uses their blinker anymore," I blurted out randomly. "It's a jungle out there, Honey."

"You know," she said seriously, "this may be one of the last things you can pass on to your daughter. In another year, she'll be off to college and living her own life."

"I have just two words for you," I said, grasping at straws. "Turnpike!"

"Stop talking like an idiot and take your daughter for a driving lesson."

CHAPTER TWO

I reassembled my car as slowly as I could. Unfortunately, by the time I finished, the sun was still up. Actually, it was only 12:45 in the afternoon. I meandered into the house like a disoriented mental patient. As I came through the front door, my daughter rushed up to me and threw her arms around my neck. She saw the panic in my eyes.

"Don't worry, Dad. I read the learner's permit handbook three times. I know it inside out."

Those simple words made me feel so much better. I looked at her lovingly. "I'm glad to see you're taking this seriously, Sweetie."

"I am," she answered confidently. "They make you read it each time you take the test, you know."

It's amazing how fleeting a moment of joy can be. I started getting a cramp in my liver. At least I think it was my liver. "You did pass the permit test, right?" I asked in a quivering tone.

"Of course, Dad. Why do you think I took it three times?—so I could pass and get my permit. Now come on, let's drive."

"I'll be with you in one second, Sweetie. I just have to touch base with your mother before we go."

As I passed my son's room, his door creaked open and he gave me a discreet nod. "Pssst," he voiced. I approached cautiously.

Without a word, he handed me a white motorcycle helmet, two kneepads, and one cracked elbow pad. With a sardonic grin, he whispered ominously, "See ya round, Dad."

I could only say "Where's the other elbow pad?" He shook his head in pity and quietly closed his door.

By the time I reached my wife, my anxiety level had reached a fever pitch. I stood in front of her with the helmet tucked under my arm, looking like a deranged astronaut. I launched into a two-minute incoherent run-on sentence. Even I had no idea what I said. She looked at me like I had just killed the neighbor with a shovel.

"Have you lost your mind?" she asked. "Get a grip on yourself. You're taking your daughter for a driving lesson, for crying out loud. You look like a condemned man walking to his execution."

At least *that* would be a happy ending, I thought miserably. I finally blubbered out a semi-lucid phrase. "Why not you teach?" I said, sounding like an Apache from a B western.

"Because I'm making dinner, doing laundry, and cleaning out that junkyard you call a closet, that's why," she said. "Give me those things. Come on, hand them over. You can't get in the car wearing that stuff or else she'll lose all her confidence."

"Can I at least bring my pistol?" I asked pitiably. I figured if things went really bad, I might be able to burrow a hole in my skull sufficient to induce a coma. She gave me a dirty look, pulling the helmet and pads from my death grip.

CHAPTER THREE

As I handed the car keys to my daughter, I swear I had a religious experience. At least that's what it felt like. Visions of personal injury lawyers, trauma surgeons, and irate insurance adjusters filled my eyes. I think they call it a waking nightmare. I climbed into the passenger seat wondering if it might not be better to sit in the back.

I yanked so hard on my seat belt that I squashed all the air from my lungs.

My daughter was smiling, happily adjusting the seat position, straightening the rearview mirror, and calmly examining the dashboard. She started the engine and slowly backed out of the driveway.

I vaguely recall the experience even though I was in an altered state most of the time. I do remember making odd sounds like "make right" and "stop sign." Apparently, I was adopting a second language: B-movie Indian. My Ford got a little roomier. It was two inches deeper at the firewall from the constant pressure I applied to it during the ride. And I knocked the heel off my shoe from something called ghost braking, which means "to slam one's foot into the firewall, simulating a braking motion."

Still, it worked out. We made it home safe with just a couple of near misses, one of which was the Gronemans' dog. I would have considered this a bonus. My daughter did much better than I anticipated. She was serious and intent during the whole affair, something I had never seen in her before or maybe just never noticed. My confidence slowly returned, and once again, I could fill my lungs normally without the use of a paper bag.

"Well, you don't look too worse for the wear," said my wife when we got home. "What's that red mark on your forehead?"

"That's what we call, in driver education, 'dashboard head,' Honey. It comes from repeated blows to the forehead while demonstrating the subtlety of slow braking. Don't worry, the dashboard's rubberized. It cleared my sinuses nicely."

SAY WHAT YOU MEAN

Jesse Neve

I HAD JUST FINISHED feeding Baby Jonathan, and he was happily enjoying one of his morning naps. My daughter, Sarah was two years old and not scheduled for a nap until the afternoon. She and I read a book together, and then I set her up with crayons to draw while I planned to quickly mop the kitchen floor. Instead, always wanting to be by my side, Sarah watched me fill the bucket with warm, soapy water. She was obviously intrigued. She stood right behind me as I started on one end of our small townhouse kitchen.

In my most stern, motherly voice, I said, "Do not put your hands in that bucket." Sarah's big brown eyes stared up at me as she nodded in compliance. She was always a good listener, so once I knew that she understood, I wasn't really concerned.

No sooner had I turned around with the mop when I heard a huge splash. Surprised, I looked back and saw Miss Sarah standing with her foot—and pants-leg, and sock—up to her knee in the bucket of water.

"It's true," I thought, shaking my head, "I hadn't said a thing about putting her foot in the bucket." She had done everything I had asked.

Well, There Goes My Dignity

Christina Gochnauer

T O REALLY UNDERSTAND THIS story, you need to understand a few things about my family first. All of my kids are
adopted. The relevance here is that I didn't know better because I
hadn't been a parent for years prior. While most families start with
one teeny fragile baby, ours started with the one teeny fragile baby
girl and fragile, too-tiny eight- and nine-year-old boys.

You also have to understand that I am absolutely overconfident
in my ability to control the chaos. Nine years into this parenting
journey, I still think I can do the impossible: make everyone happy
and get out of the store with what we need and only what we
need. The difference now is that I know how to prepare better
and try to avoid taking all the kids to the store at the same time.
I was still a brand new foster parent the day of "the incident," and
my overconfidence was trumped only by my sheer exhaustion and
absolute belief that I was going to be great at this whole thing.

My kids came to us with next to nothing. My husband had
unfortunately been scheduled to go out of town the day after the
kids arrived. But remember, I'm still in my stupid phase. The "I
know better and can do this better than anyone ever" phase. I had
so many ideas about how to do this thing right. I don't know where
that confidence came from. It certainly wasn't earned.

The first issue was getting the kids loaded into the car. Car
seats are tricky things if you don't know what you're doing, and
I certainly did not. The fact that the boys were unable to contain

their excitement about going to a store should have been an omen of things to come. I thought it was an exaggeration when they said they'd never been in a store before.

We unloaded from the car with very little issue. I plopped the baby in a baby sling across my chest and grabbed each boy by a hand. The older of the two insisted on walking in front of us, and rather than fight, I allowed him to do so—that is, until he almost walked into a car that was backing up. I grabbed his arm and hauled him back to me so as to prevent him from being hit by another car. He was so offended by the fact I touched him—and dared to move him without his permission—that he didn't talk to me for several minutes and spent most of the trip looking like an angry Snoopy.

I should have gone back to our car and gone home then. But now I was determined. We were at the store, and by golly, we were going to buy what we needed! I told the boys that if they kept a hand on the cart and didn't fight, they could have a treat at the end. I didn't specify what the treat would be, which . . . my bad. Obviously, I should have been more clear.

We walked all around the store, grabbing toothbrushes, tooth-paste, pajamas, underwear, breakfast cereal, kids' shampoo, and various other things. When I was satisfied with what was in the cart, I told the boys we were going to the candy aisle to pick their treat. This, dear reader, would be my biggest mistake.

Their little overstimulated brains saw the candy and went berserk. Suddenly it was as if we were on an episode of Supermarket Sweep. I watched in horror as they began to pelt bag after bag of candy into the cart. I told them to stop, that they were only getting one. But they either couldn't hear me in their excitement or simply chose to ignore me. When there was no more room for candy to fit, they finally stopped. I told them again, only one bag—put the rest back.

The older boy's face fell, but he began to put bags of candy back on the shelf. The younger one, though . . . you would have thought perhaps I had just inflicted a fatal blow. In the span of about ten seconds, he was lying on the floor, flailing his limbs in what looked to be a mime's version of a temper tantrum. He wasn't making any noise, just kicking and hitting anything around him he could reach. After a minute or two, I told him to get up so he could pick his candy and we could check out. He refused to budge. And so I ended up doing something I'm still ashamed of. I picked the kid up surfboard-style, told his brother we were leaving right now, and started marching toward the exit.

So now there was an enraged child under one arm, a baby who had just seemed to realize something was wrong and began fussing on my chest, and a now-distraught nine-year-old boy wailing about how unfair it is that he can't have candy, he's starving, I'm mean, and on and on. And while this was all happening, I seemed to have gathered a bit of an audience. The stares of judgment were awful. And of course, no one offered to help, but one "helpful" person suggested the eight-year-old was too big to be carried. To be clear, I absolutely agree—he was very small for his age but still weighed enough that I was getting uncomfortable carrying him. But shouting that at me when three out of three kids were in obvious distress was not the most helpful thing in the world.

When we finally made it home, I asked a friend to go to the store and see if she could find the cart and check out for me. She did and all was well. But still . . . I don't take them all to the store if I can help it.

House-Showing Fiasco

Amilee Weaver Selfridge

ONE NIGHT AFTER OUR two young children went to bed, my husband and I were enjoying some quality time together . . . on our phones. Like many nights before, my husband started showing me the dream houses on Zillow that he thought we should move to. Only this time when he showed me a house, instead of laughing at him, I surprised him by saying, "Let's do it!"

We can be impulsive and don't like to waste time. So less than twenty-four hours later, we saw the house, found an agent, and put an offer on it.

Unfortunately, red flags popped up during contract negotiations, so we backed out. But the idea of a new house stuck. We pressed forward, again wasting no time. Within the next week and a half, we visited twelve more houses, put an offer on a house, had that offer accepted, signed a contract, and now only had four weeks to sell our current home *and* move.

No problem . . . right?

While my husband worked full-time, I began the arduous challenge of selling our house and packing, all while taking care of two young boys.

Thankfully, we had several interested buyers request showings. All I had to do was get the house clean.

To clear some of the mess, I started haphazardly throwing belongings into boxes—which, of course, seemed to always fly straight back out at the hands of a curious child. I would clean one mess just to turn around and see two more.

As time crept on, I was getting more and more stressed. What on earth had we gotten ourselves into?

Again, I would clean and clean. Find more messes. Repeat.

We were down to one last hour before it was time for the showings.

I was so close.

I was walking down the stairs when I looked toward my kitchen. Separating our front room and our kitchen, there was a pony wall—one of those pointless shorter walls that doesn't reach the ceiling—and it was *so* dusty and dirty on top. There was no way I could leave it for the showings.

My youngest son needed to be fed before I could get it done. But I was confident I could accomplish both tasks in time for the showings.

My son does not eat by mouth. Because of physical and mental challenges, he eats fully by G-tube, a tube that enters directly through his stomach, bypassing his mouth. We place the formula in a machine, which then pumps it directly into his stomach. Feedings this way are time-consuming, so we put his machine in a little backpack he wears while playing. Cute and efficient.

I got my son's feeding set up, climbed a ladder, perched atop the four-foot-wide wall, and started cleaning.

Minutes later, my older son told me the floor was wet. I ignored him.

A few more minutes passed and my son told me the couch was wet now too.

Finally registering what he said, I looked down to see that my younger son had removed the feeding tube from his stomach and it was now leaking all over the front room.

A giant vanilla-scented mess.

I quickly turned to climb down the ladder to stop the flow of food, when . . .

The ladder disappeared!

My older son, desperate to help me during this crazy moment, accidentally knocked over the ladder.

Here I was, on top of a tall—and yet somehow not tall enough—wall. I had one child running around the room leaking formula all over the floor and furniture, another child standing in the corner crying because all he wanted to do was help, and the clock quickly ticking down the moments until potential buyers would walk into this mess. What was I supposed to do?

Really, there was only one thing I *could* do: jump.

I did my best to gather my nerves and moved closer to the couch. Hopefully that would soften my fall.

Then I jumped!

Ouch.

Seems I miscalculated life—again. I landed on the hard floor covered with toys. Not even close to the couch I aimed for.

There was no time for pain. Moving faster than should be possible at that moment, I got moving. I stopped my son's food from splattering every surface in the house, used my beloved carpet cleaner to clean the spills, and prayed the visitors would think the lingering vanilla scent was a candle. All the while, both my sons screamed and cried in the background.

With only minutes to spare, I grabbed what I needed and headed to the car with my boys. While running down the stairs to head out the front door, I skidded to a stop.

That pony wall.

I never finished it.

In fact, I made it *way* worse.

Now the top of the wall was half-cleaned, leaving the other dirty half glaringly, obtrusively obvious.

Time was out. I had to leave it.

We went to the car to drive around the neighborhood during the showings—not wanting to go too far, because, of course, I *had* to stalk our potential buyers.

Only, as we waited, no one came.

Thirty minutes, an hour, two hours.

The first showing group never showed up . . .

(Kids crying in the car.)

The second showing group never showed up . . .

(Kids crying in the car.)

The third showing group never showed up . . .

(Kids crying in the car, begging to go home.)

Finally, the fourth showing group showed up.

I was so happy I was going to cry! (We're pretending like I wasn't already stress-crying right along with my boys.)

But the group never went into the house.

My phone vibrated, and I looked down to see a text from our agent: "The fourth showing group has decided the neighborhood does not fit what they are looking for and they are going to pass. "

The group pulled away from my house, taking with them the last bit of my sanity.

Sore and tired, I walked back into my house and just sat there.

Even my boys deflated, seeming to understand it was all for nothing.

With perfect timing, my husband walked in the door from work, eager to hear how everything went.

He took one look at our exhausted faces, one sniff of the vanilla aroma, and said, "Oh no. What happened?"

A few weeks later, as we sat amid piles of boxes in our new house, all we could do was laugh. It was six weeks to the day from when my husband routinely showed me a pretty house with no intention of it going anywhere. Though the days were easy to count, the number of fiascos we had and tears we spent during that time was too high to count. But we survived it. And now we were home. With lots of new crazy days to laugh about for years to come.

Gone Rogue

Viji K. Chary

S OME OF MY FRIENDS think I run a tight ship because of the house rules I enforce on my children. But I think the rules are reasonable. They stem from a work-before-play philosophy.

One Saturday, I went to an all-day writing conference. That morning, my friend came over to find my son playing video games. Shocked at the scene, she asked my husband where I was.

"She's gone to an all-day writing conference," he answered.

The scene now made sense. I would have never let my son play video games in the morning had I been home. Dad was in charge.

The day went on.

I finished my conference and came home to find my children working diligently on their homework.

"What wonderful children!" I cooed.

Both my son and daughter tried to hide their laughter.

I looked at my husband for an explanation. "I told them that you were going to be home in fifteen minutes and that they should look like they've been working all day," he confessed.

"So they've done nothing productive all day?" I asked.

He shook his head.

I sighed. They had had a free day. But I wasn't upset because I knew I was the taskmaster parent and my husband was the easygoing one. In the end, children need both kinds.

The Three Most Dreaded Words in the English Language: "Some Assembly Required"

Gary D. Koppel

THERE ARE THREE TYPES of men: men who don't need directions, men who follow directions, and me.

Full disclosure: You will never see me shopping at IKEA. The problem with IKEA is that all their furniture comes in a flat box—*with directions*! And to make matters worse, the directions do not include any words whatsoever—just simple, cartoon-like pictures to guide you through the assembly process.

I must admit, even if they had included written instructions, it wouldn't have made a bit of difference. I simply do not understand, nor am I able to follow directions. It's just not part of my brain chemistry. If I need someplace to store my books, I'll do what I did when I was in my twenties: get some two-by-fours, grab a few cinder blocks from some construction site, place the said two-by-fours on said blocks, and then . . . with nothing but the aid of gravity . . . voilà! Bookshelves. That is the extent of my handiwork.

Added to this fact is that I'm not particularly handy with tools. *Not handy with tools?!* That's an understatement. I'm lucky if I can actually name maybe three or four tools. Hammer. Wrench (I think). Screwdriver. Oh, and get this—as it turns out, there's more than just one kind of screwdriver. Who knew?

And for your information—FYI, I'm more of an "FYI guy" than a "DIY guy"—I simply lack many of the skills for the "manly arts."

And I have absolutely no shame about this. I have no need to prove that I am a real man.

Nonetheless, the one manly art that I *am* proud of is being a single father. For that, I did not need a lot of direction. It just seemed to come naturally to me. I'm also especially grateful for having a daughter, as this relieved me of the burden of having to teach a son how to hunt, fish, or use power tools.

In any case, despite my best efforts, there were two areas of expertise over which I had absolutely no mastery, and in which no amount of direction was going to help. First was combing my daughter's hair when she was a little girl. Occasionally, I would be able to tie her hair back into what was supposed to look like a ponytail. Thankfully, each morning when my daughter arrived at preschool, one of the moms, with brush in hand, would rush over and suddenly become her personal hairstylist. This daily "makeover" made all of us happy. As they say, "It takes a village."

The other area of my incompetence is with any toy that comes with directions.

So it's Christmas Eve, and my daughter is finally, *finally* asleep, I take that as my cue to begin creating the most *perfect* Christmas morning ever. I don't remember if "the stockings were hung," but the milk and a half-eaten cookie were in place, and for my Oscar-winning "special effects" moment, I leave some of Santa's "boot prints" on the carpet. I was good to go.

But as I'm stacking the presents under the tree, I suddenly get the horrifying news: *Barbie's Townhouse: Some assembly required!*

What? Oh no! Now what? What am I going to do? The only thing I *could* do. In the words of Frank Sinatra, I did it my way.

Was it a total disaster? Let me just say—if the building inspectors had shown up, they would have red-tagged it immediately. Just to get the house to stand up at all, I had to find a piece of string and then tie that string from the second-story window of the townhouse to the leg of my dining room table. So much for perfection. The clock was ticking.

Christmas Morning: My daughter bounces out of bed, races to the living room, and then . . . just stops . . . cold. Frozen in place. Speechless. Motionless. She looks around, taking it all in. And then I hear three of the most *magical* words ever uttered in the English language: "*He was here!* Dad, look! He was *here!*"

Oh, and FYI . . . sometimes the only direction you need is to follow your heart. No assembly required.

You Can't Make This Stuff Up

"We literally have nothing to eat."

Pure Honesty

Jesse Neve

M Y HEART DROPPED WHEN I heard the voice of my son's third-grade teacher on the answering machine. Why was she calling me? Her message asked me to stop by and talk to her in the morning when I dropped Daniel off for school. This couldn't be good. I asked Daniel what she might want to speak to me about, and he couldn't think of anything out of the ordinary that had occurred recently.

We arrived at school a little bit early the next day and made our way up to his classroom. We were greeted warmly by Ms. Kotila, who we had known forever. In fact, she had been Daniel's preschool teacher too.

"I just wanted to let you know that Daniel's science test grade is going to look a little lower than you're used to. It was a really hard test, and everyone did poorly on it. I allowed everyone to do test corrections on it, but Daniel chose to only make one correction when he turned it back in."

Our eyes turned to Daniel for an explanation.

With pure, childlike honesty, Daniel looked up at us and said, "Well, I read over the problems that were marked wrong, and I thought, 'No, these are right. Ms. Kotila must be wrong.' So I left them."

We both just stared at him in amazement. Had he seriously just told us that he thought his teacher had incorrectly scored his paper?

Both Ms. Kotila and I were trying to keep a straight face for Daniel's sake. She quietly explained to him that, in the future, if he thinks she has made an error, he should bring it to her attention quietly and she can check her work. That way, he could still get the points if he wanted to change the answer. He agreed in a businesslike manner.

Later she told me, "Wow, that kid has guts to call his teacher out like that! I almost wanted to give him the points just for being so brave and confident in his (wrong) answers!"

The Storyteller

JB Polk

ONE OF MY FAMILY'S classic Christmas movies is *Christopher Robin*, the heartwarming tale of how a grown man's midlife crisis is solved by talking to a stuffed bear. It reminds me of my father, a "Christopher Robin" all his life. And by that, I mean he was a man who loved honey and had that lovely albeit peculiar habit of talking to animals—stuffed or otherwise.

Dad's been my superhero who could find the TV remote faster than anyone else in the house. But he was also so ridiculously talented that he painted like da Vinci (minus the fancy beard), could fix a car tire with nothing but glue (who needs a spare tire anyway?), and played any instrument without even bothering to learn music. We'd hand him an accordion or a keyboard, and he'd figure them out in about ten seconds and then play any tune like . . . Mozart on steroids. At least that's how it seemed to my six-year-old eyes.

But most importantly, my father knew how to tell stories and had a knack for coming up with the wackiest titles. We're talking gems like "The Epic Tale of How Your Sister Broker Her Thumb Chasing Squirrels," "The Time I Almost Became a Human Pretzel," and of course, "The Legendary Banana Peel Disaster That Ruined the Family Picnic." Trust me, our family gatherings were never dull! Every story was bursting at the seams with more plot twists than a pretzel factory (no relation to Dad's "almost" condition), characters so vibrant they could be mistaken for a box of crayons, and life lessons that clung to your brain like gum to a shoe.

But let me tell you about "The Synchronized Family Puke"—a real masterpiece of eeriness!

My dear old Dad loved to regale us with tales of his childhood in Poland and the country's food shortage after World War II. Imagine living in a world where everything is as scarce as blue unicorns, and in a desperate quest for food, Poles had to resort to reaching out to their long-lost relatives who had managed to escape the chaos before the war. They'd send their sob stories to places as far-flung as the United States and Australia and, in return, received Spam, oatmeal, pickled herring, and lime Jell-O. Dad's family survived the first postwar year in this manner.

Now get this: My dad swears that a mysterious package appeared on their doorstep out of nowhere. And what was inside, you ask? A box with a medium-sized jar, complete with a screw top and absolutely no label. My grandmother, a master (or *mistress*, to use inclusive language) of creativity, cracked open the container only to find a substance that resembled powdered milk but in a dim and flavorless shade of gray. (Yes, she even dared to taste it with her finger!) Being the genius she was, she concluded that it must be a protein booster and promptly started adding it to the family's soups. Everyone was overjoyed with the extra calorific contribution until—talk about timing—the jar had hit rock bottom, and a letter from my grandmother's brother arrived.

"Dear Sister, I've sent over the 'Wife-in-a-Box' crematorium ashes edition. May she rest in peace and not cause any spooky shenanigans! All she ever dreamed of was a cozy little spot next to her dear old mom. I pray you grant her last wish, giving her that magical send-off!" Dad said the words read to that effect.

According to Dad, the clan engaged in a coordinated regurgitation routine for a week, with dear auntie finding her final resting place in the porcelain throne. It seems evident that eating members of one's own species is illegal, yet no one can be held accountable if they are unaware of it, especially if it gives them a bout of indigestion!

But then I can't help but wonder if Dad's story is reliable at all, because guess what? My sister broke her thumb trying to skip a rope, *not* chasing squirrels. Who needs squirrels when you can have a broken thumb, right? As for dear old Dad, he didn't "almost" transform into a human pretzel, but he did manage to sprain his ankle while practicing the mystical yoga "Destroyer of the Universe" position.

It looks like Dad might have taken his storytelling skills to a whole new level, adding some extra sparkle to make the tales as thrilling as a roller coaster ride. But then, maybe they did devour my aunt by the spoonful . . . I'll never know now because Dad, who is no longer with us, has taken the secret with him.

A Fast Excuse

Tammy Brown

M Y SON, WHO WAS about ten at the time, came into the house wearing an exclamation point.

Slam!

The door was his first victim.

Bam!

The floor became his second as he threw his backpack on the ground.

"Carson, calm down. What's the matter?"

Carson had indeed had a bad day, and he immediately began giving me the ugly details.

He was so irate, however, that he must have forgotten who he was talking to. Every other word was an expletive as he angrily explained the day's events. I didn't like hearing my ten-year-old curse, but I thought I would address that issue after Carson calmed down.

In the middle of his rant, he must have realized that he was venting to someone who could ground him because he stopped mid-sentence. His eyes widened, and he became quiet.

I could almost see the wheels turn in those few seconds of silence, and his mood changed once again. His eyes dropped and his shoulders slouched at his best attempt to look meek.

He innocently looked up at me, batting his baby-blue eyes, and said, "Mom, I think I have Tourette's."

My laugh started with a chuckle and then grew into a roar. My giddiness scared Carson at first because it meant I didn't fall for his excuse. However, he eventually joined me in laughing at this brilliant white lie.

Our joviality was so strong that it almost completely washed away my son's bad day. And I never did scold him for his choice of language. With an excuse that good, I thought he earned a get-out-of-jail-free card.

THE SOCIAL WORKER'S SHOES

Frances Gaudiano

"I'M AFRAID WE'VE EXPLORED every avenue. There is no specific reason you can't conceive. You're probably just a bit too old."

I didn't say anything, embarrassed by the tears falling down my face. Of course, I was too old. What had I been thinking?

"You could try IVF, but the odds at your age aren't good."

I blew my nose and stood up, murmuring 'thank you' though it was beyond me why I was supposed to be grateful for being told I had geriatric eggs.

"Would you be okay with me taking hormones for IVF treatment?" I asked my husband when I got home. "I might have mood swings and become irritable at times."

He abruptly left the room. I took that as a no—that and the fact that he got his suitcase out of the loft.

I decided that adoption would be a safer option. Again, I queried my husband. "What if we adopted?"

He pondered a long moment. "I'm not sure I could love someone else's child."

"You love your dog and we didn't give birth to him!"

My husband looked at the dog and had to agree with me. I contacted the local council and told them we were interested in adopting.

Their first question was, "Can you supply your age please?" I wanted to reply *not dead yet*. We were too old to apply for an infant

213

but might qualify for an older child. But I wanted a baby—a child who didn't already have a name and a history that would need managing.

At that time, China had a surplus of baby girls. I had just watched the Olympics and fell in love with the Chinese girls' gymnastics team. They were so cute! Aware that this was a stupid reason to adopt from China, I bought a few books on China and an introductory manual to Mandarin. I styled myself as a Sinophile to impress the interviewing social worker.

Once we had a date for our interview, the cleaning began. Floors were scrubbed, windows cleaned, questionable souvenirs hidden away, controversial novels hidden. The nursery was painted a lovely lilac color, and a few children's books were tastefully displayed on the dresser. The dog was bathed. The carpet was bathed. I had my hair cut and tried on various cosmetics to make me look younger. (Not much success there) My husband even got a new shirt.

The fated day arrived. Mr. Simon came to the door with a briefcase. "Would you like me to take off my shoes?" he asked.

"You don't have to. Well, maybe after we've been in the garden."

Mr. Simon was impressed with the greenhouse.

"We love gardening!" I exclaimed. My husband gave me a look. This was only the second time I had ever visited the greenhouse. I ignored him, turning to Mr. Simon. "We can't wait to plant things with our child. Learning about nature is so important." Mr. Simon made a note on his clipboard. I grinned at my husband and gave him a thumbs up.

On re-entering the house, Mr. Simon left his leather brogues next to our boots, and we gave him the full tour. The nursery was examined for health and safety concerns (all sockets covered, window lock on) and then we sat down for the full interview. The dog wanted to join in the discussion, but I was afraid he would get up on the sofa (which could be deemed too unhygienic by social services) so he was placed in the kitchen.

"I'd like to ask you some questions about your family relationships," Mr. Simon stated. "How did you get on with your parents?"

My parents were dead, so I got on with them just fine. "I would love to have my mother around to give me advice. She was a fantastic mum. I miss her every day."

"And your father?"

I smiled. "He was a real character."

My husband didn't have it so easy, as his parents were alive and he's an honest person.

"Do you practice any religion?" The pen was poised over the clipboard. Which was better, being religious or not?

"Lapsed Catholic," I confessed, "but I go to church at Christmas, and I think children should know something of the Bible. I mean, it's mentioned in literature a lot." I was floundering. I turned to my husband.

"I used to be a Buddhist," he offered.

"Oh, that's good," Mr. Simon replied. "It's one of the predominant religions practiced in China." It seemed like my husband was scoring all the points. First the greenhouse and now the Buddhism.

Mr. Simon looked up from his clipboard, "How is the intimacy in your relationship?" Silence. "Would you like to discuss this separately?"

"I'll make tea." Fleeing to the kitchen, I put on the kettle, ate a few chocolate biscuits to calm my nerves, and then returned to the lounge. My husband left then, and I heard him talking to the dog. Would that be counted against us? Is it bad for children if their parents talk to the dog?

I had no idea what I said in my private interview but was relieved when my husband returned.

"There's one issue we must discuss because you're adopting from another country. How will you deal with racism?" We both stared at Mr. Simon. "For instance, if your daughter were teased at school, how would you respond?"

Why, I'd give the other child a good wallop. I almost said. Wrong answer. I let my husband field this one.

"We'd have a quiet word with the teacher and maybe the parents of the other child." I tried hard to not raise my eyebrows at his explanation. Quiet—yeah, right.

Mr. Simon stood up then and shook our hands. It would take a few weeks for him to write his report, but he thought everything looked good. I let out a huge sigh.

"We do have to follow procedures in order to maintain the safety of vulnerable children." We agreed and led him to the hallway. He reached for his shoes, but they weren't there.

"I'm sure I left them here."

I looked at my husband, who glanced down the hall toward the kitchen, where the dog was.

"Finley?" he asked. Finley came bounding up to us, the tongue of a leather brogue hanging from his mouth. I leaned against the wall, trying not to faint. My husband left in search of the rest of the footwear. He returned with one mauled shoe and another that was basically a sole and nothing more. I waited for the social worker to pull out the clipboard and write a big red X across our application.

Mr. Simon placed one foot in the tooth-marked but intact shoe and then the other on the forlorn sole. Thinking better of it, he left the remnant and gathered his things to leave, wearing one shoe and just a sock on the other foot.

"I'm so sorry," I whimpered, and then Mr. Simon began to laugh.

"It's a pair of shoes. We can't measure a child's life against a pair of shoes."

We adopted our daughter a year later.

Tooth Fairy

Fiona M Jones

F OR A FEW SHORT years, I was a tooth fairy, a collector of tiny pearls. I wasn't very good at it.

The job description is simple enough. The teeth have been yours all along. You have watched each one emerge from grumpy pink gums; you have counted them and brushed them with the softest toothbrush and the mildest toothpaste; you have let them snarl at you and bite on your fingers; you have watched them wobble and loosen. You know when and where each tooth lies under which pillow, for you practically placed it there yourself. And you're fully intending to harvest and treasure two tidy little sets of twenty perfect teeth.

My problem is, I'm far too absent-minded. In the morning, a warm, reproachful squidgelet would climb onto me and complain that the thing I'd promised hadn't come to pass.

"Oh . . . don't worry," I would say. "Sometimes it takes more than one night. Just leave it there until the tooth fairy comes along."

"The tooth fairy better remember," said the squidgelet, fixing me with a determined pout that he clearly intended for an authoritative frown. "Or I will be cross, Muppy."

"Okay, okay, she'll remember," I promised, with obvious guilt, and I put the coin ready beside my own toothbrush so I couldn't forget again.

I performed my duty carefully for the next few teeth, enjoyed my children's patronizing approval, and watched my little collection of baby teeth gradually grow. Of course, both children knew the tooth fairy was a story, and I was fairly sure they could see I was aware that they'd known that from the start, but I gather they rather liked the feeling that this was one game they played better than Muppy did. They wouldn't beat me at chess for another ten years at least, but already they had me cornered at Tooth Fairy.

The game lasted, profitably enough on both sides, until one of my sons decided it was time to revise the terms of the deal.

"Muppy," he announced, "I don't believe in tooth fairies, but I'll still have the money, and I want to keep the tooth myself as well."

I nodded. I had to. It was checkmate.

And that is why I don't have a full collection of baby teeth. They are scattered now, in among toy cars and plastic bricks, lost among the other debris of childhood. In the end, I'm glad I wasn't the one who lost them.

Mom

Karl Stevenson

I T WAS 7 A.M. on a Tuesday morning and I was twelve years old, back in 2007. I was at the point of maturity where I was trusted to begin my day in solitude but needed a once-over by my mother to ensure that I was set to get on the bus. For breakfast, I made an omelet filled with pepper, bologna, and cheese as an accompaniment of MTV music videos played in the background. My mother finally emerged from the hallway in a black muumuu, with rollers barely clinging to her hair. I glanced at the clock—8:05 a.m.

Normally around this time, my mother would ask me if I had all my books, make sure that my shoes matched, and watch me as I left for the bus stop. However, she was distracted by her current weight loss journey, so I just hung out at the dining room table while I waited for the bus to arrive.

The bus driver I had throughout the majority of my public school experience was a woman I respected. Ms. Oak would punctually arrive at my stop at 8:15 a.m. and would greet each child with a smile, but she also ensured with an iron fist that no one was harassed or bullied by another student. Now, I'm not saying that my bus driver would ever hit a child or apply any physical force, but . . . she had a tendency to approach whoever was being problematic and "accidentally" fall on them. (And she was *not* a petite woman). Ms. Oak also wouldn't tolerate any extreme name-calling or verbal harassment—while driving, she would gladly call out a child and indirectly insult them to end it.

It was finally 8:10 a.m. I put on my shoes and grabbed my backpack. My mother finally decided that today was ab day. She moved the coffee table back, loosened her bra, and went to light a candle to cover the impending smell of sweat. The poor Bath & Body Works candle she chose for the day was a favorite of hers. The wick was all the way at the bottom and there was ash around its opening.

To compensate for the lack of lighting surface area (on the wick), my mother grabbed some pages of yesterday's newspaper, crumpled them up, lit one end, and tried to light the candle. I guess the breeze from the front door being opened killed the flame instantly, so she had to up her game. I watched as my mother grabbed an arsenal of newspaper and hairspray . . . and something in my gut told me I needed to take a few extra steps away from her. When she lit the chemically drenched wick and paper, flames shot up higher than when the firework blasted Shan Yu in *Mulan*. She quickly put on oven mitts and found the fire extinguisher, rushed over to grab the candle, and headed straight out the front door.

My stomach dropped as the school bus stopped in front of my house while my mother fought flames in her black, sweat-stained muumuu, hair curlers dangling in the wind, and her bra at her ankles. I heard Ms. Oak tell the kids to stop trying to take pictures, but I could see her chuckling too as she pulled the bus away from the curb.

MOM-RADAR

Jesse Neve

T HE SUMMER MORNING HAD been busy but usual. Breakfast dishes were just washed, and I had already completed two loads of laundry. I picked up one-year-old Ben as I walked through the main floor, subconsciously doing a headcount.

Three-year-old Daniel was working with the fire trucks in the living room. I didn't see or hear my "old" kids anywhere (ages five and six). I set Ben down next to Daniel, who instinctively passed Ben a fire truck that he himself wasn't interested in, in the hopes that Ben wouldn't "steal" his favorites. Immediately Ben started squealing his "siren" and driving the truck across the carpet to the "fire." I hopped over the wooden stairway gate, a successful maneuver that I completed dozens of times each day but that visitors struggled with in awe.

As I neared the top of the stairway, I found that the door to the bedroom that Jon and Daniel shared was closed. That alone was a suspicious situation, and a red flag instantly went up on my Mom-Radar. A crayon-written note in Sarah's handwriting was taped to the door. It read: "No buddie come in this room. We are NOT trying to get into the attic."

Hmmm . . .

If Someone Offers To Help You

Kathleen Vacek

"I F SOMEONE OFFERS TO help you, have them carry your bags, not the baby."

I got this text from my mother-in-law as I was leaving the house. The baby gear, the stroller, the baby, the passports, and my giant backpack were loaded in the car.

Oh, Grandma. I rolled my eyes. Kidnapping was not one of my worries.

At the airport, I strolled up to the ticket counter to check in, confident I had all my international travel ducks in a row. I had notified the airline that I would have a baby with me; I knew I had to pay his international departure tax. I was ready.

"Hmm . . ." The young white man working the ticket counter kept his eyes on his computer monitor and clicked things. While he tried to figure out how to charge me for the departure tax, the other passengers all boarded the plane. The flight was being held for us. The agent gave up and told me to board—no tax was paid. I wrangled the stroller and backpack and passports through the now-empty security line and boarded the plane.

Whew. We made it. Not the smooth start I'd expected, but all would be well now.

Shortly into the flight, with Jonathan on my lap, I rubbed his back through his cotton onesie. My hand stopped, feeling something warm and wet. Liquid poop oozed out the top of his diaper and seeped through the onesie. I changed the diaper and his entire outfit in the tiny airplane toilet, jiggling with mild turbulence—the first of several blowout diapers en route to Toronto.

Thankfully, Jonathan was a happy baby despite the trouble with his bowels. He nursed and slept and played and smiled. I calculated how many diapers I had left before I had to buy more. I had booked an Airbnb with a washer and dryer, close to a grocery store, so I could buy diapers and wash his clothes and pack just a backpack for the two of us.

We touched down in Toronto. As we strolled down the jet bridge, I got out my cell phone to call the car service I'd booked. Knowing I would not be able to carry a car seat while pushing the stroller and handling travel documents, I had scoured the internet for a Toronto car service that supplied car seats. I dialed the number. No service. Hmm. I tried again. No service.

My stomach dropped to the floor of the jet bridge as I realized my phone did not work in Canada. I had failed to set up a plan for mobile service during the trip.

Yet I had a voicemail that must have come through in flight, before crossing the border, which I listened to while pushing my baby in the stroller through the airport.

"Hi, Kathleen. This is your Airbnb host. I'm so sorry, but I'm being evicted from my apartment and the locks have been changed, so you won't be able to stay here. Here's the number for Airbnb customer service."

I gripped the handle of the stroller and my heart pounded even faster. No Airbnb. No phone to contact Airbnb or my car service. Before I could solve either issue, I had to get through customs. When it was my turn, I approached the cubicle and passed my documents through the slot at the bottom of the window. The agent eyed me warily and looked closely at my passport, the baby's passport, and the notarized letter from my husband granting permission for me to travel outside the country with our son. Jonathan started to cry. My brain was awash in cortisol. The agent stamped our passports and waved us through.

With Jonathan crying in his stroller, I began searching for a way to make a phone call. Amazingly, I located some pay phones near baggage claim. First, I called Airbnb. My hands shook as I rolled the stroller back and forth with one hand and held the heavy, black pay phone handset in the other. Voice wavering, I relayed the message from my Airbnb host to the customer service rep. "I have my baby with me," I squeezed out, blinking back tears.

The customer service rep was upbeat. "Not to worry," he said, "We have you booked into a hotel for two nights. Then you can pick another place for the rest of your trip. Here's the address of the hotel."

Okay—our immediate need for shelter was solved for now. I called the car service, finally. As we waited for the car, I calmed Jonathan down. We got to the car. The driver, a polite and professional middle-aged man with brown skin and thinning black hair, presented me with the car seat and reminded me of the company policy that the parent, not the driver, install it. I struggled, of course. Anyone who has ever tried to put a car seat in a car knows what a nightmare it is. The driver broke the rules and tried to help me. Still, the car seat felt loose, and as we whizzed down the highway in Toronto, I held on to it, as though that would prevent critical injury if we got in an accident.

I needed to call my friend who had traveled to Toronto from Montreal to babysit Jonathan while I was giving my conference presentation. I needed to tell her I was not staying where I thought I would be. But I didn't have a working phone. The driver let me use his. I knew my friend would not pick up a call from this unknown number, so I left a message. We arrived at the hotel, and the driver deposited the stroller, the baby, the backpack, and me on the sidewalk. The car pulled away, but before I could make it through the hotel's glass doors, it came back, and the driver ran up to me with his phone.

Thank God. Brianna had called back. I told her where I was and why I didn't have a working phone and what a mess this whole day had been.

My baby and I checked into the ridiculously hip boutique hotel and rode the elevator up to our room. I collapsed on the bed, crumpling under the pressure of all that had just transpired. Jonathan crawled on the floor, finally released from his stroller. I wanted to cry, but I still had problems to solve: the phone, housing beyond the next night, the diapers, and the dirty laundry. I retrieved the tablet I had packed from the backpack and got on the hotel Wi-Fi. I got through to T-Mobile customer service and paid for a Canada plan for my trip. I called my husband and listed off the disasters one by one.

Brianna and her boyfriend arrived at the hotel. I hadn't met Max before; he graciously left us alone so Brianna could console me. Later, they took all of Jonathan's poopy clothes back to their Airbnb to wash them.

The modern bathroom was all glass and white tile glistening under recessed lights. I filled the enormous square tub from the faucet in the ceiling. Jonathan splashed around in it, grinning at me with a gleam in his eye that said, *What an adventure, Mom!*

When I submitted my proposal for the conference, I had a tiny baby—my first, obviously. The conference date was just after his first birthday. *By the time the conference comes around, this will be so easy!* I thought. I may have been working on my PhD, but this was not a smart move. *If someone offers to help you* . . . have them carry your bags, the baby, *and* you. Then buy them dinner and a really nice beverage to go with it.

PARENTING IS A TRUE ADVENTURE INDEED

Amilee Weaver Selfridge

SOME MIGHT SAY THAT parenting is not the most adventurous life. Earlier nights, less romance, fewer heart-pounding thrills . . .

Most likely, though, they just haven't had the chance to enjoy the thrill, romance, and adventure of parenting themselves.

I want to tell you a tale of parenting that includes it all: late nights, romance, *and heart-pounding* thrill.

Those with sensible tastes or weak hearts might want to close their eyes and skip this story—lest the thrill prove too much for your delicate soul.

One evening, my husband and I began our normal bedtime routine for our two children. We got our oldest son ready for bed, then went to our youngest son's room to get him ready as well.

In his bedroom, there hung a climbing ladder from the ceiling—a toy for him to climb and swing on.

In the few minutes we had left him alone, he got fully undressed, climbed to the very top of the ladder, and had what can only be called an extremely explosive accident. Explosive enough to not only cover every rung on the ladder but also two beds, a window, a recliner, a mini-tramp, an opened toy chest, and even the ceiling. Rather appalled, my husband and I just stood there, not fully knowing what to do, until our son started trying to lick the ladder. At record speed, we braved the mess to get him away from the ladder.

You would have thought that with two adults and one small child, this would be a simple task.

You would have thought wrong.

Minutes later, all a little worse for the wear, we finally pried his hands off the wet ladder and pulled him away, forcibly transporting him to the shower.

We got him sprayed down, scrubbing all the poop off (which, of course, he found completely hilarious, laughing his head off the whole time).

I left my husband with the laughing little monster to go clean the room, only to find our dog in the middle of the mess—eating it! I yelled to get her to stop and looked up to see our oldest son standing there laughing.

Then, straight out of the mouth of babes and completely dead serious, he says, "Don't worry about me, Mom. I'm not going to try to eat it too. This looks like a *huge* mess. Why don't I put myself to bed so you can clean it up?"

And he did. He turned straight around and walked to his bedroom without another word.

A couple of hours later—after 9 p.m., I'll have you know—my husband and I sat on the mostly clean floor, surrounded by trash bags, disinfectant, and carpet cleaners. We toasted our love and the thrill of the evening spent together, clinked our cups of milk together, and then each popped some ibuprofen into our mouths.

Proof that you can still have late nights, romance, and heart-pounding thrills even when you have kids. Parenting is a true adventure indeed.

THE VERDICT

"Your Honor, in the matter of do your kids make you old or keep you young, the jury was unable to reach a verdict."

Acknowledgements

It feels only fitting to start the acknowledgments of a parenting book by reflecting on parenting itself.

Parenting was the spark that inspired me to start *The Bad Day Book* series. As a mom, I wanted to share my stories in a way that brought laughter and connection—without sounding like I was complaining too much. Parenting is undoubtedly an adventure, full of (often funny) bad days, but no matter how many bad days we face, I wouldn't choose any other way.

So, my first thank-you must go to my two sons. Without you, this book—and this series—wouldn't exist. You are my inspiration and my constant chaos. Some days, I feel like I can't live with you, but I could never survive without you.

A giant shoutout to my parents—for teaching me to walk, talk, and eventually adult (well, sort of)! Thank you for loving me, tolerating me, and never disowning me—despite everything. You are truly heroic.

A heartfelt thank-you to the incredible contributors and authors who joined me in sharing their stories. This book is a collective labor of love, and it wouldn't have been possible without your willingness to share your experiences, humor, and perspectives. Thank you for enduring the countless bad days we faced while creating this project—both from the parenting perspective and the publishing perspective!

To my editor, Liz, who stepped in late in the process and brought this project to life with incredible talent and dedication—thank you for your hard work and for being such a joy to collaborate with.

To my cover designer, Jenalee, who has been with me since the very beginning—thank you for crafting a design that captures the spirit of this book. We all know people judge books by their covers, and your fun and vibrant design has made this one truly stand out.

Lastly, thank you to the cartoonist who brought a unique depth and perspective to this book. Your ability to capture the essence of parenting in a single image is nothing short of amazing, and your illustrations have added a layer of humor and relatability that words alone couldn't achieve.

If we have to live with the chaos of parenting, at least we can find comfort in knowing we're not alone—and that's exactly what this book is all about.

Artists

Ali Solomon: *Now That I Finally Have It All. I'd Like to Give Some of It Away.*
Al Rozanski: *Chess with Child*
Frega Diperri (Nathan Diperri & Julianne Frega): *Mommy, I Want a Snack*
Jonny Hawkins: *Parenting Mystery, Mom Wanted Her Hair Dyed*
Philip Witte: *How Does She Do It Without Help*
Samantha Lau: *My Toddler Learned the Word Why*
Sarah Morrissette: *We Literally Have Nothing to Eat*
Steve Delmonte: *Tip the Firemen*
Suzy Becker: *Parenting Sins, Happy Meal, Parenting Verdict*

Authors

Amilee Weaver Selfridge, who provided 10 stories, including *House-Showing Fiasco* and *If You Only Knew*
Anna Remennik: *Slice of Life*
Annette L. Brown: *4 Shots + 1 Needle = a Surprise*
Bien Santillan Mabbayad: *Sing with Your Heart*
Christina Gochnauer: *Well, There Goes My Dignity* and *Why I'm Not Allowed in The Pet Store Anymore*
Dave Bachmann: *The Pinata*
Devin A. Reese: *Multitasking Blues*
Don Drewniak: *The First Day Accident* and *The Fortune Teller and the Kid*

Ed Meek: *Reading Aloud*
Erika Hoffman: *Pretty, Productive, and Tomato-like* and *Vigilant Grandma*
Fiona M Jones: *Tooth Fairy* and *Visiting Time*
Frances Gaudiano: *The Social Worker's Shoes*
Gail Collette: *White Water Canyon Kids*
Gary D. Koppel: *The Three Most Dreaded Words in the English Language: "Some Assembly Required"*
Heather G. Preece: *I Will Find You Pee Smell*
Jan Cauffiel Zinn: *To Lie or Not to Lie? What a Question!*
JB Polk: *The Story Teller*
Jennifer Companik: *A Dangerous Thing I Brought on an Airplane*
Jesse Neve, who provided 10 stories, including *Say What You Mean* and *The Lone Shoe*
Jessica Marie Baumgartner: *Locked in the Bedroom*
Jon Jones: *The Wake Up Call*
Joyce Frohn: *First Day, Worst?*
Jules Older: *Night[mare] at the Opera*
Karl Stevenson: *Cheesecake* and *Mom*
Kathleen Vacek: *If Someone Offers to Help You*
Katie Sakanai: *The Influenza Diaries*
Kay Lesley Reeves: *A Wonderful Day*
L. Jade: *Parenting Pros and Cons*
Laura Niebauer Palmer: *The Unforgettable Airport Adventure*
Lorina Stephens: *A Slippery Situation*
Mark Daponte: *Parent vs. Cellphone*
Mary Traynham: *Surviving Kindergarten*
Michele Herman: *Rain Date*
Nan McKernon: *The Name Change*
Peter Lewis Ebbitt: *Never Brake a Promise*
Robert Runté: *Of Cannibals and Mice* and *The Death of a Pet*
Rose Florian: *Kitty's Very Bad Day in the Loo* and *Steaming Apricot Soup*

Sarah Das Gupta: *A Birthday Egg*
Sarah Mallari Bucu: *Kyle's Homemade Conditioner and Moisturizer*
Sarah Meade: *Mommy Meet-Up*
Sarah Walker: *Mother's Guilt* and *One Thing After Another*
Steve Denehan: *How to Raise a Daughter* and *Cola*
Sunayna Pal: *The Standing Joke in the Family*
Tammy Brown, who provided 6 stories, including *A Quick Nap* and *The Wild One*
Tony Daly: *A Moment*
Trisha Simone: *Poop and Other Explosions*
Viji K. Chary: *Gone Rogue* and *Integrity*

THE
BAD DAY
BOOK™

-because every day needs a good laugh and a great book-

DISCOVER MORE-SCAN HERE

Website

Freebies

Podcast

Get Social

 Open The
Camera App.

 Point your camera at a
QR Code to scan it.

🌐 thebaddaybook.com ✉ publisher@thebaddaygroup.com
🌐 thebaddaygroup.com 🔗 @thebaddaybook

www.ingramcontent.com/pod-product-compliance
Lightning Source LLC
Chambersburg PA
CBHW071713140626
46557CB00011B/64